THE GREEK TRAGEDY
IN NEW TRANSLATIONS

GENERAL EDITORS
Peter Burian and Alan Shapiro

EURIPIDES: Medea

EURIPIDES

Medea

Translated by
MICHAEL COLLIER
and
GEORGIA MACHEMER

OXFORD
UNIVERSITY PRESS

2006

OXFORD
UNIVERSITY PRESS

Oxford University Press, Inc., publishes works that further
Oxford University's objective of excellence in research,
scholarship, and education.

Oxford   New York
Auckland   Cape Town   Dar es Salaam   Hong Kong   Karachi
Kuala Lumpur   Madrid   Melbourne   Mexico City   Nairobi
New Delhi   Shanghai   Taipei   Toronto

With offices in
Argentina   Austria   Brazil   Chile   Czech Republic   France   Greece
Guatemala   Hungary   Italy   Japan   Poland   Portugal   Singapore
South Korea   Switzerland   Thailand   Turkey   Ukraine   Vietnam

Copyright © 2006 by Oxford University Press, Inc.

Published by Oxford University Press, Inc.
198 Madison Avenue, New York, NY 10016

www.oup.com

Oxford is a registered trademark of Oxford University Press

Library of Congress Cataloging-in-Publication Data
Euripides.
[Medea. English]
Medea / Euripides ; translated by Michael Collier and Georgia Machemer.
p. cm. —(The Greek tragedy in new translations)
Includes bibliographical references.
ISBN 13: 978-0-19-514566-3 (pbk.)
ISBN-10: 0-19-514566-6 (pbk.)
Medea (Greek mythology)—Drama.   I. Collier, Michael, 1953–
II. Machemer, Georgia.   III. Title.   IV. Series.
PA3973.M4C65 2006
882'.01 — dc22   2005026742

Printed in Canada

For Corona Machemer and Tom Sleigh

EDITORS' FOREWORD

"*The Greek Tragedy in New Translations* is based on the conviction
that poets like Aeschylus, Sophocles, and Euripides can only be properly rendered by translators who are themselves poets. Scholars may, it
is true, produce useful and perceptive versions. But our most urgent
present need is for a *re-creation* of these plays—as though they had
been written, freshly and greatly, by masters fully at home in the English of our own times."

With these words, the late William Arrowsmith announced the purpose of this series, and we intend to honor that purpose. As was true
of most of the volumes that began to appear in the 1970s—first under
Arrowsmith's editorship, later in association with Herbert Golder—
those for which we bear editorial responsibility are products of close
collaboration between poets and scholars. We believe (as Arrowsmith
did) that the skills of both are required for the difficult and delicate
task of transplanting these magnificent specimens of another culture
into the soil of our own place and time, to do justice both to their
deep differences from our patterns of thought and expression and to
their palpable closeness to our most intimate concerns. Above all, we
are eager to offer contemporary readers dramatic poems that convey as
vividly and directly as possible the splendor of language, the complexity
of image and idea, and the intensity of emotion and originals. This
entails, among much else, the recognition that the tragedies were
meant for performance—as scripts for actors—to be sung and danced
as well as spoken. It demands writing of inventiveness, clarity, musicality, and dramatic power. By such standards we ask that these translations be judged.

This series is also distinguished by its recognition of the need of
nonspecialist readers for a critical introduction informed by the best
recent scholarship, but written clearly and without condescension.

Each play is followed by notes designed not only to elucidate obscure references but also to mediate the conventions of the Athenian stage as well as those features of the Greek text that might otherwise go unnoticed. The notes are supplemented by a glossary of mythical and geographical terms that should make it possible to read the play without turning elsewhere for basic information. Stage directions are sufficiently ample to aid readers in imagining the action as they read. Our fondest hope, of course, is that these versions will be staged not only in the minds of their readers but also in the theaters to which, after so many centuries, they still belong.

A NOTE ON THE SERIES FORMAT

A series such as this requires a consistent format. Different translators, with individual voices and approaches to the material in hand, cannot be expected to develop a single coherent style for each of the three tragedians, much less make clear to modern readers that, despite the differences among the tragedians themselves, the plays share many conventions and a generic, or period, style. But they can at least share a common format and provide similar forms of guidance to the reader.

1. *Spelling of Greek names*

Orthography is one area of difference among the translations that requires a brief explanation. Historically, it has been common practice to use Latinized forms of Greek names when bringing them into English. Thus, for example, Oedipus (not Oidipous) and Clytemnestra (not Klutaimestra) are customary in English. Recently, however, many translators have moved toward more precise transliteration, which has the advantage of presenting the names as both Greek and new, instead of Roman and neoclassical importations into English. In the case of so familiar a name as Oedipus, however, transliteration risks the appearance of pedantry or affectation. And in any case, perfect consistency cannot be expected in such matters. Readers will feel the same discomfort with "Athenai" as the chief city of Greece as they would with "Platon" as the author of the *Republic*.

The earlier volumes in this series adopted as a rule a "mixed" orthography in accordance with the considerations outlined above. The most familiar names retain their Latinate forms, the rest are transliterated; -*os* rather than Latin -*us* is adopted for the termination of masculine names, and Greek diphthongs (such as Iphigen*ei*a for Latin Iphigenia) are retained. Some of the later volumes continue this practice, but where translators have preferred to use a more consistent practice of transliteration of Latinization, we have honored their wishes.

2. *Stage directions*

The ancient manuscripts of the Greek plays do not supply stage directions (though the ancient commentators often provide information relevant to staging, delivery, "blocking," etc.). Hence stage directions must be inferred from words and situations and our knowledge of Greek theatrical conventions. At best this is a ticklish and uncertain procedure. But it is surely preferable that good stage directions should be provided by the translator than that readers should be left to their own devices in visualizing action, gesture, and spectacle. Ancient tragedy was austere and "distanced" by means of masks, which means that the reader must not expect the detailed intimacy ("He shrugs and turns wearily away," "She speaks with deliberate slowness, as though to emphasize the point," etc.) that characterizes stage directions in modern naturalistic drama.

3. *Numbering of lines*

For the convenience of the reader who may wish to check the translation against the original, or vice versa, the lines have been numbered according to both the Greek and English texts. The lines of the translation have been numbered in multiples of ten, and those numbers have been set in the right-hand margin. The (inclusive) Greek numeration will be found bracketed at the top of the page. The Notes that follow the text have been keyed to both numerations, the line numbers of the translation in **bold**, followed by the Greek line numbers in regular type, and the same convention is used for all references to specific passages (of the translated plays only) in both the Notes and the Introduction.

Readers will doubtless note that in many plays the English lines outnumber the Greek, but they should not therefore conclude that the translator has been unduly prolix. In some cases the reason is simply that the translator has adopted the free-flowing norms of modern Anglo-American prosody, with its brief-breath- and emphasis-determined lines, and its habit of indicating cadence and caesuras by line length and setting rather than by conventional punctuation. Even where translators have preferred to cast dialogue in more regular five-beat or six-beat lines, the greater compactness of Greek diction is likely to result in a substantial disparity in Greek and English numerations.

Durham, N.C   PETER BURIAN
Chapel Hill, N.C.   ALAN SHAPIRO

CONTENTS

MEDEA

INTRODUCTION

·

MEDEA IN THE MORNING LIGHT

As the sun, rising above Mount Hymettus, lights up the packed wooden bleachers on the south slope of the Acropolis, some fifteen thousand Athenian citizens and resident aliens, their retinues and guests from abroad,[1] revived by warming wine, readjust their cushions, pull their cloaks around their shoulders against the early morning chill, and gaze down at the wide circle of the deserted dance floor (*orchestra*). A short while before, just after dawn, it had been abustle with purifications, libations poured by generals — chief among them Pericles — announcements of gold chaplets (*stephanoi*) awarded to the city's benefactors, panoplied war orphans eligible for the first time to bear arms against the foe, and buckets of gold and silver tribute from subject states. But now the tribute has been removed and all the VIPs have taken their seats at the foot of the hill. In the front row, toes to the orchestra's rim, the year's most prominent office holders and other notables flank the Priest of Dionysus at the center and the ten judges, just chosen by lot,

1. Were women present? There is no good evidence one way or the other, but my guess is no, not so much because of demographics, as because of Greek attitudes toward their wives and daughters appearing in public at all and because I suspect that the satyr plays and old comedies performed along with the tragedies at this festival would have been considered too lewd for proper women to see and hear. Demographics support this conclusion: Thucydides gives figures for the number of troops, both citizen and foreign, available to Athens in 431 BC for the conduct of the war (*Peloponnesian War* 2.13), which, though hotly disputed by modern scholars, suggest that even if only half of these men (numbering in excess of 90,000) were in the city at the time of the festival and that if even fewer than a third of these attended the theatrical performances that spring day, along with their sons, others exempt from service or disabled, numerous resident aliens not serving, and foreign guests (and their servants?), there would have been scant room on that crowded hillside for proper ladies. Even the performers were men. It was almost a men-only political club at play. If women were there, they would probably not have been the chaste wives and daughters of upstanding citizens. For a good discussion of the Athenian audience at the City Dionysia, see Simon Goldhill, "The Audience of Athenian Tragedy," *Cambridge Companion to Greek Tragedy*, ed. P. E. Easterling (Cambridge, 1997), 54–68.

who will soon cast their votes for this year's winning poet (not destined to be Euripides, who will come in third or dead last). Nearby stands the old wooden statue of the wine god, brought in procession to the festival and thought to be as eager as the human spectators to watch the show. The trumpets have sounded. Anticipation has settled into stillness. In the backdrop spanning the rear of the dance space, palace doors open. The *Medea*, a new play by the notorious Euripides, is about to begin.

What did the audience expect that morning in mid-March 431 BC, as they watched a solitary man wearing the mask of an old woman shamble toward them, and were their expectations met or frustrated? How might they have interpreted the actions and the words of the masked actors and dancers—fellow citizens all—who came before them that day to sing, to dance, to gesture, to declaim, and to honor the wine god who mingled his spirits with theirs? What circumstances impinged on their consciousness? How would their assumptions and reactions have differed from ours as they witnessed the drama from whose script our Greek text, corrupted over time, is derived, a sometimes uncertain remnant of that first performance?

For months they had known that Euripides, already in midcareer, would be one of the three tragic poets exhibiting that spring at the annual city festival of Dionysus. He, Sophocles (Euripides' senior by at least a dozen years and a frequent favorite with the judges), and Euphorion (son of the great playwright Aeschylus and destined to be this year's victor), along with their respective chorus masters, the *choregoi*, had been chosen the summer before, shortly after the highest ranking city official, the *eponymous archon*, whose duties included oversight of the great festival of Dionysus, had taken office. Whatever shows the other two poets might put on, Euripides' were sure to rattle the audience, for he had been schooled by the sophists—those foreign-born, self-promoting, self-styled wise men who, with Pericles' encouragement, had arrived in boomtown Athens to peddle their newfangled, high-priced higher education to any with the leisure and means to become conversant with its confounding techniques of arguing the pros and cons of any issue and its unnerving theories about the nature of things—and he often made his characters act as though they had received the same indoctrination.

His fellow Athenians must have had mixed reactions to his characters' more extravagant sophistries. To those who were less than sanguine about the new ideas floating around Athens, who feared for the future of Athens and for their own, and who saw in Euripides' dramatic style a sign of the city's corruption, they must have been painful. How large this group was and who belonged to it we do not know. We can guess that it included those whose power and prestige was tied (or so they thought) to inherited landed estates (large and small) and who despised the manners and pretensions of newly "sophisticated" youths and their teachers and were opposed to Pericles' aggressive, populist, imperial policies; or, for that matter, just about any fathers or guardians who at home were scandalized by back-talking, rebellious sons and wards or who in the courts had been bested by captious arguments. The list was probably as long as the motives for disliking Euripides were many. Yet, despite his poor showing with the judges, the list of Euripides' fans was even longer. He fascinated those among the upper classes, especially the leisured, city-dwelling younger generation, who had imbibed the new learning at its source and were more than ready to applaud characters who thought and talked like, or more cleverly than, themselves. Even the as-yet unenlightened, less well-to-do majority, who were either too busy or too poor to pay the sophists' exorbitant fees, must have been easily seduced by rousing displays of spellbinding rhetoric unavailable to them by any other means. They were regaled by characters who might at any time begin to wax philosophical and question the veracity, worth, even the existence of the Homeric gods and whether men ought to be worshiping them, and, if not them, who or what.

But to these working men, better than all the logic-chopping and philosophizing was the way Euripides brought the imposing presences from Greek myth—those lofty alter egos of Athens' proud, Spartan-loving oligarchs—on stage in, shall we say, debasing circumstances. His characters, less remote, more human, delighted the newly enriched and newly empowered lower classes—city-dwelling, landless traders and artisans who had prospered from the manning and maintenance of Athens' large navy and from the new markets Athens' supremacy at sea had opened up. Thanks to Pericles, who for the last dozen years or so had been the undisputed master of Athens, and much to the chagrin of the so-called few (*oligoi*), aristocrats who thought themselves more qualified by birth and upbringing to rule, these vulgar many (*demos*), whom Pericles had flattered, rewarded, and led, now dominated the assembly and the courts. It must have been they most of all who a few years back had applauded so wildly when, dressed in rags, the great and noble son of Heracles, the Mysian Telephus (in a lost Euripidean play of that name) had hobbled before ancestral Argive peers to beg for aid. Surely there would be more outrageous surprises of this kind from Euripides' fertile mental store, something everyone could love hating.

They will not be disappointed. In the play they are about to see, the wondrous, magical, triumphant marriage of two matchless heroes — Jason, captain of the Argonauts, and Medea, his trophy wife — will enter the divorce court. To an audience raised on Aeschylus's larger-than-life personages, the leading characters of the *Medea* will seem disturbingly like the chattering high-folk of imperial Athens, whose dirty linen, though washed, has been hung out to dry. Under Euripides' tutelage, the art of masking is being transformed from a ritual putting-on of the real presence of a god or antique hero into the presentation of a familiar type confronted with familiar situations. As exotic as Medea is, she is still a woman; as unusual as her story is, it is nevertheless the story of a marriage; as assimilated to the divine nature as her sorcery is, for an ancient Athenian it still rings true to the real-life activities of lady herbalists or "root-cutters." Yet, although Euripides' protagonists will suddenly seem a bit too uncomfortably familiar, the play will be no *Who's Afraid of Virginia Woolf*. The action will remain public — there will be no displays of unseemly misconduct in the women's quarters — and, by our standards, the diction will seem grave, discreet, and declamatory, though the question of carnal attraction, in keeping with the mythical tradition, will not be altogether avoided. It is mentioned in the prologue (7–8) and emerges prominently as an issue in several of the choral odes and in Jason's caviling.

Not only have the spectators that morning long been expecting something shockingly sophisticated from Euripides, they have also been primed for a "Medea in Corinth." On the day preceding the grand procession that inaugurated the five-day festival, at a preliminary ceremony in the Odeion, the new auditorium flanking the Theater of Dionysus on the audience's left, each competing producer had first presented his poet, his chorus of fifteen men, his actors — also men, usually limited to three, the number necessary to play all the roles throughout the play by assuming different masks — and then announced the subjects and settings of the four plays his team would soon present — as a rule three tragedies, followed by a ribald satyr play (a burlesque of heroic myth in tragic style). Though they held celebratory garlands, the performers were maskless and wore ordinary dress in place of the elaborately embroidered "royal" robes or lewd satyr costumes they would don for their performances. That year Euripides would be offering the *Medea*, along with three other plays now lost: a *Philoctetes*, a *Diktys*, and a satyr play called *Theristai*.

LEGENDARY BACKGROUND

Ancient Greek myths tend to coalesce around ancestral dynasties, in this case, around one known as the Aeolidae, descendants of Aeolus,

Jason's great-grandfather, who had originally ruled in the plains of Thessaly in northern Greece. One of Aeolus's seven sons, Athamas, had two famous wives. The first, Nephele, bore him a son, Phrixus, and a daughter, Helle; the second, Ino, attempted to kill Phrixus. In fifth century accounts of this wicked stepmother's plot and its thwarting—we know of at least three plays of Sophocles and three of Euripides that touch upon it—there seems to have been an abortive sacrifice of Phrixus, after which he and his sister fly off toward the East on the back of a golden ram, sent either by their mother, Nephele, or by a god. Helle falls off, giving her name to Helle's sea (the Hellespont), but Phrixus arrives safely in the land of the Colchians at the eastern end of the Black Sea. Here he sacrifices the golden ram and gives its fleece to Aeëtes, son of the Titan Helios (the Sun) and King of Aia, a city on the Phasis River. In return, Aeëtes welcomes him into his household and gives him the hand of a daughter (Medea's sister) in marriage. After fathering a number of sons, Phrixus dies in Colchis. All this time the unearthly fleece hangs in a sacred grove, safeguarded by a huge serpent.

Meanwhile, back in Thessaly, the scene has shifted to the harbor town of Iolcus, at the foot of Mount Pelion. Athamas is no longer in the picture, and his nephew Aeson, the father of Jason, has been overthrown by Aeson's half brother Pelias. At the time of the coup, Aeson's supporters entrust the boy Jason to the wise centaur Chiron, who raises him far from town in a cave near Pelion's peak. Years pass. Pelias, though tormented by a prophecy to beware of a man wearing a single sandal, rules without opposition. Then, one fine day just such a one-sandaled man arrives in Iolcus: a heroic figure, indeed, in Pindar, who a generation earlier wrote:

> a man terrible with twin javelins; and a twofold guise was on him.
> A tunic of Magnesian fashion fitted close his magnificent limbs,
> and across it a panther's hide held off the shivering rains.
> Nor did the glory of his streaming locks go shorn,
> but blazed the length of his back. Striding apace
> he stood, and tested his unfaltering will
> in the market place that filled with people.
>
> They knew him not; yet awe-struck one man would say to another:
> "This cannot be Apollo, surely, nor Aphrodite's lord,
> he of the brazen chariot. . . ."
> (*Fourth Pythian Ode*, 78–88, tr. Richmond Lattimore)

The man is Jason, come home at last to claim his royal birthright. Along the way he has lost one of his sandals. The lines from Pindar, representative of a tradition familiar to Euripides' audience, allow us to see what that audience would have realized at once: just how far Euripides' Jason has fallen compared to Pindar's godlike warrior.

When King Pelias learns the identity of this awesome, one-shoed stranger, the wily usurper is ready with a deft proposal: The ghost of Phrixus has been haunting his dreams and has called upon him to bring the fleece of the golden ram back to Iolcus. Would Jason be enterprising enough to wrest it from the formidable Aeëtes? Jason, a hero to his core, accepts Pelias's challenge and calls upon most of the heroes of the age to go with him to the world's eastern edge, a mysterious, potent, sacred spot, charged with danger, where the Sun rises from his Underworld home, and where no Greek had gone before. They come from all over, these brave adventurers. With Athena's help, they build the world's first man-of-war, the Argo, and from Iolcus they sail (and row) into untested waters beyond the Bosporus. On the way, they encounter many obstacles, all of which they overcome, only to find the greatest obstacles of all in Colchis.

As soon as the purpose of the Argonauts' mission is made plain to Aeëtes, the ungracious and devious king sets tasks for Jason to perform in order to win the Golden Fleece—tasks that Aeëtes believes will be impossible. The hero must plow a field with fire-breathing bulls, sow dragon's teeth in the furrows, and kill the fully armed warriors that will sprout from this sinister seed. The gods, however, are on Jason's side. Aphrodite makes the king's daughter Medea fall so madly in love with the beautiful Greek stranger that she, a priestess of Hecate and therefore accomplished in the secret arts of magic, gives him potions to protect him from the bulls' fire and sound advice on how to set his new-grown adversaries to fighting among themselves. When her father does not keep his side of the bargain and refuses to grant Jason the Golden Fleece, she helps her lover seize the prize from under the watchful eye of its guardian dragon and then escapes with him aboard the Argo. Along the way, she and Jason kill her brother and, according to at least one fifth-century account (though not attested by Euripides), chop up his corpse and scatter his limbs behind them as they flee, in order to delay her father's pursuit.[2]

At some point in these adventures, in return for her aid and to protect her from her father's vengeance, Jason solemnly swears to make Medea his lawful wife. This marriage—one of the great marriages of myth, in which the human and the divine worlds come together to

---

2. Michael Collier incorporates some details of this version at lines 160–62. Euripides, however, tells us nothing about the cause or the manner of this murder, only that it was shameful (160/166–67) and that it took place at Medea's father's hearth (1308/1334).

celebrate an extraordinary union — is accomplished either on the homeward voyage, during which Medea's magical powers often come to the aid of Jason and his crew, or upon the couple's triumphal return to Iolcus. In Apollonius of Rhodes' *Argonautica*, an epic written about a century and a half after Euripides' *Medea*, it forms a highlight of the last, culminating book. Significantly, Apollonius has it take place in Phaeacia, the enchanted land where Odysseus in Homer's *Odyssey* was finally rescued from the sea and sent home to Ithaca. The marriage bed of the god-blessed couple — so often referred to in the play — was, we are told, set up in a sacred cave and covered with the Golden Fleece itself: "Nymphs gathered flowers for them, and as they brought the many-coloured bunches into the cave in their white arms the fiery splendour of the fleece played on them all, so bright was the glitter of its golden wool. It kindled in their eyes a sweet desire. They longed to lay their hands on it, and yet they were afraid to touch it. . . . As for his bride, the place where the pair were brought together when the fragrant linen had been spread is still called the Sacred Cave of Medea."[3]

The quest for the Golden Fleece had many sequels. The oldest and most famous was the murder of King Pelias by his daughters, who were tricked by cunning Medea into killing their own father, a tale that is introduced as background in the prologue of the *Medea* to account for Jason's and Medea's status as exiles from Iolcus (see notes, lines 8–9/ 9–10). Another sequel, her stint in Athens with King Aegeus, which is anticipated in the third episode of the play (658–815/663–823; see below) and set after Medea's flight from Corinth, may well have been devised only in classical times. Both Euripides and Sophocles are known to have written undatable lost plays called *Aegeus*. But even if one of them included Medea in its plot, and that play was produced before our *Medea*, it is unlikely that the Athens episode, in contrast to the murder of Pelias, would have formed a part of the audience's assumptions or expectations.

HISTORICAL BACKGROUND

Because the dates of most of Euripides' surviving plays are unknown, and because those that are known do not always belong to moments in Athenian history as well documented as the spring of 431 BC, we are not usually in a position, as we are with the *Medea*, to explore the

3. Apollonius, *Argonautica*, lines 1143–48, 1153–55, tr. E. V. Rieu (Penguin 1971), 178. For a complete account of this and related legends, see Timothy Gantz's *Early Greek Myth* (Johns Hopkins, 1993), where a valiant attempt is made to sort out the many competing versions.

relationship between the action of the play and the events of the world. The *Medea* was produced during the incidents described in the first two books of Thucydides' history of the great Peloponnesian War. Of course, that proud morning the audience did not know what the future would bring or that the war upon which they were embarking would be twenty-seven years long and ultimately disastrous for Athens. They did know, however, that it had already begun, for the previous summer Sparta had declared war, and as soon as the campaigning season got under way in earnest, efficient, ruthless Spartan phalanxes would be marching toward Athenian territory.

Anxious though the majority in the audience must have been about this anticipated invasion, chances are at least one of them, the leader of the anti-Spartan, prowar, expansionist, democratic faction, was outwardly calm, for he had already decided that such an incursion would be of little long-term consequence. Pericles had always aimed for Athens' preeminence in Greece at Sparta's expense, wanting to pit his city's young sea power against the other's venerable land power. Now his efforts were paying off. On his advice, Attic farmers, the mainstay of the heavily armed infantry (the hoplites), would soon send their livestock to neighboring islands and, abandoning their holdings in the countryside, reluctantly take up temporary residence inside the city walls, along with their women and children, their servants, and, we are told, their household furniture. Let the invincible Spartans and their Dorian allies do their worst. What had Athenians to fear, so long as they stayed behind the ramparts? With Athens' coffers bursting and her fleet unchallenged from Corcyra to Colchis, they could count on war supplies and other resources being shipped in from overseas. Meanwhile, their war fleet, manned by the best-trained rowers in the world, would make surprise raids on the inadequately guarded territories of Sparta and her allies.

In this perfervid atmosphere, names like "Argo," "Clashing Rocks," and "Corinth" were laden with implications they can scarcely have for us. Had not the citizens of Athens, like the Argonauts of old, "forced every sea and land to be the highway of [their] daring" (Thucydides 2.41, tr. R. Crawley)? Not only had they sounded the farthest reaches of the Black Sea, but with their own garrisons, settlers, and naval patrols, they had turned its once formidable waters into a large lake, from which big-bellied merchantmen, laden with grain and salt fish, made their swift, unobstructed way past the Clashing Rocks, through the Bosporus and the Hellespont, to Athens.

Athens' new prosperity and sudden power, however, had brought many problems. Foreigners, both Greek and non-Greek, had flooded the city. Many of those involved in trade, native and foreigner alike, had become newly rich and influential. As the use of ships and money increased, the land holdings in Attica that supported the hoplite army no longer counted for as much, and the room and board once supplied to farmhands and servants had given way, in the city at least, to wages. With wages came the possibility of freedom and, to the ambitious, hard-working, and lucky, social and political advancement. Old distinctions no longer applied. No one knew anymore who was who. Political allegiances shifted like sand as each man sought his own advantage.

Because tragedy by definition deals with heroes' hard times, it goes without saying that the audience that morning did not expect to see either Jason or Medea as the exultant figures portrayed in early epic or in Pindar's epinician odes from thirty years before. But what would this audience at this time have felt when they saw an old slave woman — and, as they soon learn, the slave of a barbarian princess to boot — emerge from the scene building to speak the prologue of this play? By her very appearance on stage, she immediately reoriented their expectations toward the background of the action about to unfold, toward the immigrant population growth and mixing up of peoples and status that maritime supremacy had brought in its wake. If the surviving Euripidean tragedies are any guide to the common practice of this most "democratic" of the fifth-century tragedians, then the Nurse is indeed unusual. Almost always, a god or hero speaks his prologues; she is an immigrant's slave. Oh yes, she is an aristocrat among servants (see notes, lines 1–39/1–48 and 40/49), but a servant nonetheless, and there she stands in that great circle of empty space and, like any free Athenian citizen, addresses the rulers of the sea, a symbol perhaps of the recognizable confusion of daily life in democratic Athens, where the base-born lord it over their betters and slaves and foreigners cannot be distinguished from freemen (cf. Ps. Xenophon, *Constitution of Athens*, 1.4–12).

Already nonplused by her appearance, what must their astonishment have been when the first words out of her mouth wished the Argo and its triumphs away — the Argo, whose voyage was a mythical emblem of their own sea power — and along with it the whole turmoil of domestic and public life that its sudden success had brought. Who in that audience would not have felt the pull of what she said? Even the overseas clients and the immigrants in Athens (the metics), who had prospered beyond their wildest imaginings, would have felt the anxiety of life in the fast lane, far from home and the old familiar ways evoked by this old servant's lament. But perhaps none there that day would have felt her words more strongly than the slaves, some from as far away as

Colchis, who perhaps were waiting on the edges of the crowd for the signal between plays to bring more refreshments to their masters. They too saw the veil of literary convention raised just enough to reveal a cynical reality with which they and those around them were all too familiar. Underneath the heavy veneer of the ennobling past, the commonplace was peeping through. The Argo was beached.

Then there was Corinth. Ready to pit their seamanship against that of any of Sparta's allies, how could this audience not have reacted to the drama's being set in Corinth? Although we usually say that the Peloponnesian War was between Athens and Sparta, this is merely a neat formula for a far messier reality. In reality the war arose between Athens and her allies—that is, all the subject cities of the Delian League, the maritime federation over which she ruled—and Sparta and her allies, largely the cities of the Peloponnesus, the south Greek peninsula. Of this region the chief naval power was Corinth, the northernmost city of the Peloponnesus. Straddling the neck of the peninsula, she not only controlled the north-south land route, but had once been the busiest port in Greece, until Athens challenged her ascendancy. Indeed, it was actually with Corinth, not Sparta, that the disagreements leading up to the final breach of the Thirty Years' Truce had started. Corinth was the real enemy, her fleet the real threat, her jealousy of upstart Athens the driving cause. In the months leading up to the war, Athens, already first in the Aegean and the Black Sea to the east, had deliberately challenged Corinth's control of the sea lanes between mainland Greece and the prosperous Greek colonies in South Italy and Sicily to the west. Corinth had retaliated. By the time Corinth, during the previous summer, had finally convinced Sparta, with her invincible elite land forces, to join the fight, Athens and Corinth were already fully engaged.

So, whatever his motives, Euripides had picked a myth and a setting that fit the hour. His audience, he well knew, was made up of the same citizens who had voted to aid the city of Corcyra in her rebellion against Corinth and to reject outright the last blunt, impossible Spartan ultimatum that, to keep the peace, the Athenians should give up their empire. Now, on the brink of a war they had asked for, they sat, elated and afraid, and watched Medea wreak havoc upon hostile Corinth's ruler and his new ally, the great Thessalian seaman Jason, who, fool that he was, had suddenly switched his allegiance from her to the Corinthian king Creon.

If the dramatic action had been confined to Corinth, Medea's vengeance would have been riveting, but it would have lacked the frisson generated by the sudden appearance on stage of ancient Athens' King

Aegeus offering asylum to the calculating, yet persuasive Medea (658–815/663–823). Since ancient audiences were used to etiologies in tragedy, like the one at the end of the play that accounts for the historical cult of Medea's children at Corinth, they would doubtless have been alert to the ominous etiological implications of Aegeus's ill-considered promise. Here before their eyes was a myth to explain how Corinth and Athens had become enemies. The scene thus reached out to them in several ways not obvious to us. We have no emotional commitment to Athens' founding hero Theseus, the son Aegeus is going to beget on Pittheus's daughter when he leaves Corinth; not so the Athenians, whose fathers and grandfathers had gone to great trouble and expense to bring this man's bones back from the island of Scyros to Athens and to inaugurate a festival in his honor, replete with a grand procession, sacrifices, and athletic contests. We do not sense the extent of Aegeus's blunder when, needlessly, in exchange for an heir, he welcomes Medea into his home and commits his city to her defense against her new enemies, ipso facto making them his and Athens' own, not for a single generation, but for many generations to come. We do not anticipate, as they did, that Medea will bear to Aegeus a child named Medus, who will become the founder of the ever-threatening Persian kingdom (Media), or that she will attempt to murder the noble Theseus,[4] nor suspect that the child-destroying taint clinging to her uncanny powers might still be at work in Athens in the shape of her latter-day, root-brewing disciples (see p. 19). Nor do we fear the endless inheritability of blood guilt feared by the Athenians, who, close upon Aegeus's exit from the stage in Euripides' play, discovered from Medea's own lips[5] that he and hence their shining city had made a commitment to a woman who would murder her own children, an act of pollution so dire that they might have exclaimed along with the Chorus that no ritual cleansing imaginable could make her fit to reside among them (830–39/846–55). With the full extent of Medea's plans revealed, their foreboding at the outcome of her compact with Aegeus is registered musically by the contrast the Chorus draws between Athens' glorious, god-blessed, true wisdom-engendering purity and Medea's depravity (816 ff./824 ff.). Future generations found

---

4. We know of two undated tragedies that probably dealt with Medea's attempted murder of Theseus, one by Sophocles, one by Euripides. That one of them antedates the *Medea* is proven by "a series of Red-Figure pots starting about 450 B.C. and showing Aigeus, Theseus, the Bull [of Marathon], and a woman who must be Medeia . . ." (Timothy Gantz, *Early Greek Myth*, vol. 1, p. 255.)

5. It has been concluded by many Euripidean scholars that Euripides did not inherit the myth of Medea's murdering her own children but invented it.

Euripides' lyrics the most moving parts of his plays. Was this also true at their premieres? Did the savvy Athenians, unconquered children of the gods and Earth, exult unabashedly in the glory of their city and yet fear for the danger that lay ahead? I cannot help but think so.

The audience's sense of unease at the sinister quality of the Athens-Corinth connection would have been heightened by the way in which Euripides locates the familiar political machinations of the play not in a public space but deep inside a noble house, where the destabilizing quest for personal power, honor, and glory, and for the honor of one's house, began and ended. For ancient Greek politics, as will become clearer when we look more closely at the topic of Medea's honor, was not distant like ours, representative and televised, but immediate, direct and personal, oftentimes played out among participants who had known each other since childhood. Wheeling and dealing could not be left behind when an ancient Athenian or Corinthian went home, because his home and its nexus of alliances with kin and peers constituted his faction, his party. Unstable marriage alliances and bloody vendettas (which Athenian court procedure reflected and often was powerless to replace), coups and countercoups, betrayals and counterbetrayals were the very stuff of political life throughout Greece and often undermined the common good. Not only is Euripides' play centered on one of these explosive political marriages, the maneuvering between husband and wife is brought down from the royal, public heights on which it had been displayed in other tragedies (e.g., Aeschylus' *Oresteia*) into the bathos of a domestic tug of war between a husband and his no-longer-convenient, unrestrained, foreign wife, who refuses to go quietly into the limbo to which she has been consigned and instead, unassisted, outsmarts all her pantywaist foes.

MEDEA'S CHARACTER

In developing Medea's character, Euripides plays the received tradition off contemporary situations and prejudices. Her fierce, mantic nature, to Pindar a sign of her prophetic powers (*Pythian* 4.10), is now a symptom of a defective character type: the aloof, intractable, uncontrollable, uncompromising, stubborn *authades*, who, when crossed, is given to inordinate rage and resentment and resists all attempts on the part of friends at mollification or amelioration. The Greek word is fairly new[6] and belongs to the emerging discourse of medicine, rhetoric, and

---

6. Significantly, the word first appears in the *Prometheus Bound*, which, in my opinion, is neither by Aeschylus nor much earlier in date than the 430s BC. But this is a controversial topic out of place here.

ethics, and, although rare in Euripides, is used four times to describe Medea. Up until Jason's betrayal and her unjust abasement, she had managed to conceal her true nature behind a facade of restrained solicitousness, obliging her husband and his friends when necessary (9–12/11–15) and like a true lady, showing just the right amount of reserve and dignity to make others, like the Corinthian women who have extended their friendship to her (131/138; 177–80/178–79, 181), think that she is a perfect wife — modest, chaste, and temperate (sophrosyne, or "soundness of mind/integrity of heart," includes all these attributes of a woman capable of controlling her passions, cf. line 636). But as soon as her anger is unleashed by Jason's betrayal, she starts to behave differently. Instead of passively enduring her fate, or in shame committing suicide like some wilting Madame Butterfly, she becomes totally resistant to moderation, indifferent to the propriety of her actions, incapable of bowing to the will of her betters, much less of her equals. "She is deaf to friends' advice, like a stone, like a wave" (24–25/28–29), the Nurse explains early on to the audience; and later to the Tutor, "She came into the world fierce and stubborn" (94–95/93–94); and still later to the Chorus, "She'll growl and snarl when I approach, like a lioness shielding her cubs. She'll snort like a bull. I doubt I'll lure her out" (190–94/184–89). For it is not just the violence and intensity of Medea's wrath that is at issue in the play, but its utter relentlessness, its unappeasability. Inside the house, she reveals to all her familiars that she has the reach and temper of a thwarted tyrant or of one like an Ajax or a Prometheus, who, though used to high honors, has been suddenly and unendurably shamed; except, unlike them, she has at hand the means to avenge herself upon her tormentors. Outside, before the Chorus and her other interlocutors, like a true sophist, she can play whatever role is necessary to obtain her ends, including, when it serves her purpose, that of a reserved and dignified noblewoman (semnos, cf. 222–32/214–224).[7]

Of Medea's great intellectual acumen and professional skill, Euripides' audience had no doubt. Her powers of prophecy and sorcery were essential to her mythic persona. But just as Euripides has disconnected

---

7. Even though the meaning of the opening lines of this speech remains doubtful, the underlying argument can be shown to be a ploy familiar to us from Plato and Aristotle. Wishing to disguise her true nature and forestall the accusation of authadeia, Medea insinuates that she is not really self-willed and recalcitrant as some people think but rather virtuously reserved and worthy of respect, a claim that is convincing because the simulated virtue (semnotes) is known by qualities similar to those by which the concealed vice (authadeia) is known. Thus anticipated censure is turned into apparent praise. (Cf. Plato, Phaedrus 267A; Aristotle, Rhetoric 1.9.28–32 1367a33–b27 and Eudemian Ethics 2.3.4 1221a; 3.7.5 1233b 35–38, Nichomachean Ethics 4.3.26–34 1124b17–1125a16)

Medea's passionate nature from her noble art and turned it from a virtue into a vice, so he makes his audience view her "profession," her *sophia*, in nontraditional ways. By moving her into a situation in which her political power and prestige as Jason's wife are at risk, he exposes the dark, destructive side of her talent. Like other sophists (professors, wise men) of Euripides' day, we see her arguing any side of any case that will at any given point best serve her interests. If she needs the Chorus's complicity, she obtains their good will in specious appeals for sympathy and solidarity. When her arguments fail to convince Creon that he should give her a reprieve from instant banishment, she begs abjectly for pity (abject begging was an often-used ploy in Athenian courts to arouse the pity of the jurors). Confronted by the one who has wronged her, she mounts a strong prosecution. Presented with a chance for asylum, she engages in the question and answer of cross-examination, a technique from the courts that provides the backbone of Socrates' famous method of philosophical interrogation. If upon stepping through the palace doors, she appears by turns calm and dignified, abject, confident, or contrite, she is only doing what other heroes before her had done—what loyal Greeks always still did—when confronted with an enemy. She schemes, she tricks, she deceives. Only, in this play, the enemy is her husband and his friends, and the arguments she uses are taken from the latest instruction manuals for speechmaking. Thus, those watching her proficient duplicity must confront not only the power of the new rhetoric but also a familiar truth, that when allegiances change—as they so frequently did in city politics—duplicity is a two-edged sword. Everything depends on who the true enemy—or friend—is.

Just as her transparent sophistry strips her of her inherited grandeur, so it strips her interlocutors of theirs. Thus, as she accuses or feigns submission or gloats, and Jason offers disingenuous (though, as we shall see, in real life often convincing) excuses or condescending approbation or a last, pathetic retort, he is demoted from a great hero and daring explorer to an exiled and humbled former first citizen scheming to better his lot. By the end of the play he has made such a complete mess of things and is so bested by his wife that her prediction—that he will end his life shamefully, one of the lowest of the low, a childless wretch accidentally done to death by a fragment of his old ship—is utterly believable. Nor is Jason the only character who succumbs to Medea's up-to-date tactics and cunning, although he alone exhibits no obvious, compensating virtue. By matching arguments or answering her far-from-innocent questions, both Creon and Aegeus diminish their kingly stature. Creon is less a king because, though he has taken accurate measure of his enemy, he nevertheless succumbs to her pleading and out of misplaced pity fails to make the right decision. The kings in traditional epics made mistakes, but it was the gods who befuddled their wits, not clever women and their own yielding natures. In a different situation, Creon's mildness and mercy might even be deemed princely virtues; but when his kingdom is at stake, succumbing to this side of his nature is folly; it is what Aristotle would call missing the mark most tragically.

As already indicated above, Aegeus's character is more of a puzzle, partly, I think, because, in his encounter with Medea, the techniques of forensic oratory are not being employed, and it is from the argumentative techniques of this kind of rhetoric which were being systematized in the courts that Euripides derived his technique of revealing character through dialogue. Furthermore, true to the politeness of this simpler question-and-answer dialogue, the poet chooses to make neither character say anything by way of praise or blame to the other, nor does he use a third party—a servant, a messenger, a chorus—to introduce Aegeus as he introduces Medea in the prologue. Only Medea, the prevaricator—who in the audience would take anything she says without evident rancor for Jason at face value?—has any opportunity to characterize him, and she doesn't. So Aegeus seems just, generous, and a fool; not grand but tragicomic.

Much has been made in recent times of Medea's exotic nature as a barbarian witch. Of her lack of Greek culture, considering how many important Athenians at the time were the sons or grandsons of non-Greek mothers (see p. 22), too much, I believe, has been made. The only character in the play who denigrates Medea for being a barbarian is Jason, and he, like any aristocratic student of the sophists, will use whatever convenient ploy against her he can find to justify his own actions. But nowhere else in the play does her ignorance of Greek manners or speech stigmatize her socially—in her dealings with Creon, Aegeus, or the Chorus, nor in the servants' comments—although her status as an outsider of a different kind is often at issue: as a woman who does not belong by blood to her husband's family or as the wife of a political exile who is not a citizen of the city in which he finds himself. These categories were quite distinct in the Greek mind, and in the play they are regularly signified by different words, *barbaroi* for non-Greeks, *thuraioi* or *allotrioi* for nonfamily members, and *xenoi* for noncitizens.

But of Medea's proficient barbarian witchcraft, so central to the dramatic action, moderns have made too little, or, rather, they have tended to misjudge its import. To the Athenians of Euripides' day, witchcraft was not the fantastic, pagan, sci-fi art portrayed in today's movies or on TV; it was regarded as an integral part of the latest scientific research and regularly used by proficient healers and salvific priests, whose knowledge of the demonic world allowed them to harness its forces, either to cure or destroy. Even in its most rational or materialist forms, ancient Greek science never completely separated the divine nature from the world it investigated. Essential to Aristotle's biology, developed almost a century after Euripides, was the belief that the gods are living beings and that the soul, as the vital principle governing all life forms from gods to worms, not only encompasses all our physical and mental functions but is also the very stuff—the DNA, if you will—that determines our individual natures and links us to other members of our species, both those of us now dead and those yet to be born (cf., e.g., *On the Soul* 1.1 402a ff., and *On the Generation of Animals* 1.18 724b14 ff.). To the Stoics, who came after Aristotle, the universe itself was a living creature suffused by the controlling fiery, pneumatic material they called Reason and God, and they claimed that a wise man's reason was actually a piece of this divine *Pneuma*. Such philosophizings merely rationalized an earlier, widely held, Classical belief that the human soul contains a measure of the divine, the unsullied intellect, and because of it we are in some sense akin to the gods. The greater the intellect, the more godly its possessor, and those with the most powerful, most agile, most refined minds[8] were deemed to be gods, not necessarily gods of the highest order, not the Olympic or heavenly gods who dwell in perpetual bliss, but powerful, almost indestructible beings nonetheless, the kind called *daimones*, those invisible natures proficient for good or evil who, with countless companions, travel in the soul-rich air around us, or inhabit the flowers, trees, and rivers that spring from the immortal earth, or, indeed, who themselves arise from the earth out of the corpses of previous generations or descend from on high into this miserable, tainted, mortal sphere of war, disease, decay, and death to mediate between us wretches and those glorious, uncontaminated souls above.

Although in Euripides' day this vision of the world and the role of the divine nature in it lacked the coherence of later philosophical systems, it was, nevertheless, already present in embryonic or, as late Platonists would insist, oracular form; and Euripides himself was

8. Though only implicit in Collier's translation ("And you, yes, you have a mind for plots and treachery," 537–38), in the Greek text Jason explicitly refers to Medea's mind as subtle (or finely threshed, *leptos*, 529), a word that in the late fifth century was often associated with sophistry and in Aristophanes, specifically with Socrates (and Euripides). See p. 19.

caught up in the early stages of the great intellectual task of its artic-
ulation. He was, by all accounts, associated with the most advanced
thinkers in Athens, in particular with Socrates, who was periodically
accused on the comic stage of helping him write his innovative and
disturbing plays. Whatever one may think of Aristophanes' historicity,
his unforgettable portrayal of Socrates in the *Clouds* (produced within
a decade of the *Medea*) as the archetypal priestly sophist, swinging aloft
in his basket and mingling his finely threshed, elevated thought with
the ever-flowing numinous Air, clearly relies on a popular conception
of contemporary wise men, who were laying claim to an intelligence
above that of ordinary mortals and to direct contact with divine. Even
Plato, Socrates' greatest apologist, depicts him in a similar state of intellectual communion with the divine nature. What is more, in the
Symposium, he makes the young Socrates the disciple not of a sage but
of a sage-ess, the plague-diverting priestess Diotima (*Symposium* 201D).

To this seldom-witnessed distaff side of the new schools of the
learned, Euripides' Medea, priestess of Hecate and sharer in the goddess's most secret treasury of transforming drugs and charms, surely
belongs. She is, to be more specific, a professional healer (and harmer)
trained in the art of gathering, preparing, and applying drugs. Because
this art depended upon knowledge of certain divine rites and charms,
some of which were revealed only to women, women held a secure
place in this branch of knowledge. They were thought to be particularly
capable in the nocturnal collection of roots, leaves, flowers, and bark
and in turning their finds into efficacious salves and potions, which
they must have supplied to physicians like Hippocrates (a contemporary
of Socrates and Euripides) or to less reputable healers, and which they
themselves must have prescribed, particularly in their duties as
midwives.

Like the sophists remembered in our ancient sources, holy wise
women must have wielded sufficient power through their arts to have
been labeled dangerous, *deinai*, an adjective that can describe anything
alarming but in the fifth century came to be attached to those ingenious few who were possessed of intimidating new intellectual and persuasive powers. It cannot be accidental that this adjective is often pred-
icated of Medea in the rising action of the play, where she is presented
both as the awe-inspiring, semidivine ancestress of female pharma-
cists—a being that is *deine* in the old sense of the term—and also as
her own glib, modern incarnation. She has, as it were, a split personality, and it is this unresolved tension between the exalted, awful being
who can do what her modern counterparts claimed to be able to do—
control nature—and a more mundane, more desperate, more human

reality that makes her endlessly fascinating. She is both a steward of sacred magic and a purveyor of marvels, an emblem of the times.

There are many clues throughout the play that Euripides means his audience to see Medea and her wisdom in this way, but these will not be obvious to Michael Collier's readers, because, in order to make Euripides' difficult Greek accessible to contemporary, English-speaking readers, he necessarily recasts the passages that most reveal the scientific-sophistic issues: the first three choral odes and the prologues to Medea's first two speeches. Since it is impossible in a general introduction to examine all of these, I will consider but one example, Medea's second speech (313 ff./292 ff.). Modern philologists steeped in Socratic lore have long recognized the similarity between Medea's answer to Creon's indictment (303–12/282–91) and Socrates' protestations in Plato's *Apology* that he is misunderstood and not really so wise; but not seeing its appropriateness to her character, they have treated this point of the play as a rather undramatic intrusion of Euripides' own voice, laden with frustration at the uneducated obtuseness of his audiences.

In her speech, Medea's aim is to blunt Creon's fear that she will inflict some irremediable harm upon his daughter, but rather than try to deny the truth of the inflammatory and now public fact that she is, as he alleges, "distressed at being deprived of [her] man's bed" (286) and has been "threatening . . . to take action (*drasein ti*) against [all three parties to Jason's new marriage contract], the grantor, the groom, and the bride" (287–89), she astutely prefers to answer the less pressing charge that she is "by nature (*pephukas*) wise/skilled (*sophê*) and versed (*idris*, an unusual, poetic word) in many evils (*kakôn pollôn*)" (285). Even in these few lines, the directness, imagistic force, and colloquial smoothness of Michael Collier's translation are self-evident. Instead of impeding his verses with Euripides' awkward legal formalities quoted above, he encapsulates in one or two image-laden words the gist of Creon's accusations: Medea "sting[s] with loss" (305); she makes "the darkest threats . . . against his house" (307–8); her "nature, clever and vindictive, thrives on evil" (304–5). Since the last of these three charges is the one Medea answers, but is the first to be uttered by Creon, in order to preserve continuity, the phrase "a woman like you," which echoes the idea of Medea's nature, is added to Creon's last sentence (311) as a convenient thread for Medea to pick up at the beginning of her rebuttal, when she exclaims "A woman like me!" (313). The transition is seamless, but the original line of argument is lost. The issue is no longer the frightening effectiveness of Medea's talent for and skill in the art (*sophia*) of black magic, but a more modern issue, the denigration of a clever women. Yet it was Medea's science, not just her intellectual agility, that concerned Creon, and it is this objective reality, in the guise of the new learning and its practitioners, that Medea addresses in her rebuttal. Here, with true sophistry, she turns herself into a victim of the prejudice widely incurred (in Athens) by the *sophoi*.

> Not now for the first time, but often, Creon, has my reputation harmed me and caused great evils. A sensible man (*artiphrôn pephukas*) ought never to have his children too highly educated [in the new sciences] (*perissôs ekdidaskesthai sophous*), for, apart from fecklessness,[9] their only profit is the ill will and envy of their fellow townsmen. For, if you proffer new discoveries (*kaina sopha*) to benighted bunglers (literally "left-handed," *skaiois*), [by them] you will be thought ineffectual and not really competent (*sophos*).[10] But if in the city you are thought superior to those who think they are experts (know something abstruse, *eidenai ti poikilon*), [to these] you will seem offensive. I too share in this misfortune. Being skilled (*sophê*) [in my art/science], I am envied by the latter and deemed too steep by the former. (292–305)

Instead of calling attention to her proven and therefore dangerous skill in witchcraft and its possible application to the case at hand, Medea shrewdly speaks of the *sophoi* in general, claiming, with a wonderfully personalized and, under the circumstances, apt rhetorical ploy (I wouldn't want my children to be wise), that experts and scientists like her are misunderstood. Since the majority of citizens don't know what to make of them and cannot use their advice, they are in effect useless to the city (and therefore not dangerous); at the same time they arouse envy in those who think that they too know something worth attending to or paying for. Either way, out of envy or misunderstanding, their skill is (unjustly) condemned as dangerous and deemed a potential source of trouble to the well-being of the city.

Although the Greek is not entirely clear here and the passage has in fact proved a stumbling block to exegetes, it is obvious from this rendition that Medea's arguments have nothing to do with the distinction between men and women that resonates so forcefully with us moderns and upon which Michael Collier's translation depends; rather, they aim first at the conflict between newfangled science and received wisdom;

9. Cf., e.g., Aristophanes, *Clouds* 334.

10. Twenty years later in the *Thesmophoriazousae*, Aristophanes makes a pretend-Euripides parody these lines ("For if you proffer new insights [*kaina sopha*] to the benighted, you expend them in vain [lines 1130–31]), only in the comedy the unspecified benighted being referred to here is made flesh and blood on stage in the shape of an uneducated policeman, a Scythian archer and public slave, whose pidgin Greek (in the preceding dialogue) has already assured the audience that Euripides' clever arguments will be lost on him.

then at disparities between those who are both gifted and educated and the stupid and ignorant—or, as students of Classical rhetoric know, between the upper and lower classes; and, finally, at the sometimes vicious rivalries among those competing for political prominence. All three motifs are at work here.

MEDEA'S HONOR

As telling to Euripides' audience as her sophisticated learning (*sophia*) and her unbending refusal to be placated (*authadeia*) was Medea's "divorce" from Jason and consequent reduction in legal standing from wife to concubine. The topic had been rendered thorny for many in Euripides' audience by a restrictive citizenship law ushered through the assembly twenty years earlier by Pericles himself. Previously, a child was considered legitimate if he was the offspring of a legitimate marriage and if his father had citizen status. Even many highborn, celebrated Athenians had non-Athenian mothers. Cimon and Themistocles, heroes of the Persian wars, had Thracian mothers, and Pericles himself was the great-grandson of Agariste, daughter of Cleisthenes, tyrant of Sicyon. Now both parents, no matter how well born, had to be able to prove their citizen status.

For many Athenians this law must have had grave consequences. Despite its not being retroactively applied to citizens already registered with their precincts (*demes*), it must have immediately affected young men eighteen years of age who were just then applying for citizenship. Children of Athenian fathers who were declared illegitimate lost not only their citizens' rights but their inheritances as well, which would go instead to the nearest legitimate relative and his heirs. A poor man who had little to leave his sons would not have had to defend his own or his heirs' legitimacy in court against would-be heirs or beneficiaries; a rich man was an easy target, so like most of the legislation of the Periclean age, as a rule this law punished the propertied classes more than the working man.

Another of the law's consequences must have been that Athenians who had married foreign women now had to replace them with Athenian wives if they did not want their future sons and daughters to be bastards. These divorces would have created a class of newly disfranchised, but still free, foreign-born grass widows, who, Medea-like, either had to stay in a reduced condition as concubines in their former husbands' households—the option Jason seems to envision for Medea—or find new partners and legal protectors (*kyrioi*) among the foreigners who resided in Athens or, like Aegeus in Corinth, who were just passing through.

If these independent, foreign women happened to be beautiful, rich, well-connected at home, or highly educated, they might have been seen by many powerful men as desirable additions to their households. Pericles himself might have married his notorious Milesian mistress, Aspasia, had he been able. But ironically, because of his own citizenship law, unlike the noblemen of preceding generations, he was forced to make other arrangements. What he did might seem shocking to modern sensibilities, but makes good sense in light of Athenian custom. As his Athenian wife's guardian in law, he divorced her by arranging a new marriage for her with an acceptable new husband — one wonders how much this unnamed woman suffered from the humiliation of being transferred from Pericles to someone else — and then lived openly with Aspasia as his legal concubine. Under this arrangement, their children would be free but not citizens, a fact that would not have been a hindrance to Pericles since he already had two legitimate sons by his former Athenian wife.

As for Aspasia, concubinage with Pericles brought her as much honor as she could hope to claim in Athens. As a foreigner, she had none of the public religious duties and enjoyed none of the privileges accorded great Athenian ladies. Even though within Pericles' household she might have been in charge of the domestic servants and the storeroom, as the mother of a bastard (she had one son, named after his father), she was second-class, not the equal of the proud mothers of Athenian boys. Philosophers may have admired her, but from the moment she caught her man, this influential, unconventional woman became a lightning rod for Pericles' political enemies and grist for the comic poets' mills, a convenient instigator of all his blunders and hated policies. Like Medea, she was a liability if she proved to be too much for the man who had put his honor on the line to win her.

At the time Euripides was composing the *Medea*, general awareness of the effects of Pericles' marriage law must have been quite acute, because first sons of marriages made immediately subsequent to its passage were just now applying to their precincts for entrance onto the citizen rolls. It is not surprising then to find traces of its impact in Euripides' dramatization of the appalling end of Medea's fairy tale marriage. Has not Jason, like so many Athenians, set aside his marriage oaths and dishonored his wife for his own political convenience, apparently believing that, under altered circumstances, the gods would allow his new arrangements to override old oaths (494–96/492–94)? Does he not believe that unrestrained rulers — like Creon and himself or, in democratic Athens, the majority of the citizens' assembly — could with their decrees, newly inscribed on mere wood and stone, override old unwritten marriage settlements, sanctioned not just by mouthed formulas but by oaths spoken directly from the heart to the ears of the gods?[11] To the extent that the *Medea* engaged such issues, it offered its audience small consolation that there might be satisfactory solutions. Indeed, one of the things that is so disturbing about this play is that Medea refuses to go along with the little arrangement between Jason and Creon to sustain Creon's family's rule in Corinth and to return Jason to power in Iolcus, managing instead to enforce divine justice within a single day.

The audience that morning in the Theater of Dionysus must have begun to squirm in their seats when Medea and Jason finally confront each other in the great debate (*agon*) that supplies the climax to the first part of the play. In the course of her argument, Medea reviles her former husband for his contempt of their marriage contract, his willingness to trample her honor, and his desertion of their friendship, not in the emotional sense so much as in the sense of an alliance of interests. To satisfy his lust, a man had other places to go, but for the raising of chaste and strong children and harmony within the house, tranquil friendship (*philia*, the word Aristotle uses to describe the relationship between man and wife) was best. Medea's lust, her succumbing from the outset to the strong and wrong Aphrodite (cf. *Medea* 634 ff./627 ff.) in her relationship with Jason, was a sure sign of something gone awry in the marriage she had forged in defiance ironically, of all the old unwritten laws of the family she now invokes; it is a sure sign of a force that might in the end tear a friendship apart (cause civil war), rather than cement it for all time. For in this society, where all friendships were understood to entail a mutual exchange of benefits, not just goodwill rooted in affection, and every party to a friendship was publicly judged according to the amount of honor he had gained in forging it, a dishonoring misstep could lead to disaster.

When Medea says to Jason, "Or have the gods allowed you / to make new rules that govern oaths?" (495–96/494), her meaning for the ancient audience was far more pointed than it is for us modern readers. When she says, "Come then, if you want, I'll speak to you as a friend and ask the questions a friend would ask" (502–4/499), she means what she says not just in an intimate, personal sense but in the wider political sense upon which their union was founded, as a wartime alliance between herself and Jason. In fact, however, she had been willing to betray her father's house, not for gain—as Jason liked to think—but for love. She was so maddened by love, so innocent of Jason's true

11. Cf. Sophocles, *Antigone* 453–55; Plato, *Phaedrus* 274B ff.

character, that she told herself it did not matter that she was marrying him for the wrong reasons and in the wrong way. But, of course, in the delicate balance of honor gained and given, it did matter. She gave up the rights that she held under her father's rule for other rights, secured, she thought, by oaths; but as it has turned out they were rights that could be overridden as soon as the political winds shifted.

Although Jason's arguments in his defense may seem lame and chauvinistic to us, who feel the justice of Medea's charges, they were probably familiar to Euripides' audience and would have had more force with them than they have with us, because Athenians had both used them themselves and believed them implicitly. Like Jason, Athenians might have argued that, since emotions did not count, according to the public honor code, a foreign "wife" actually got more out of her friendship with her Greek husband than she had put into it. Just the chance to live in Greece so far exceeded her investment that she would have no grounds for complaint. Through her Greek spouse, she, like Medea, would have achieved celebrity and the privilege of submitting to Greek "laws" rather than barbarian force. The irony of this latter claim would probably have been felt by Euripides' audience, who were increasingly aware of the way Athenian laws, not least the marriage law, could be imposed on others, both individuals and subject city-states, by whoever at the moment ruled the assembly. The decrees they voted upon every month seemed to undermine the ideal of inherited law and to serve convenience rather than justice. Thus, in the play, when Jason alludes to the privilege of living under Greek laws,[12] which kind did they think he meant, the sacrosanct traditional laws that Greeks were willing to die honoring, as the noble 300 Spartans had done at Thermopylae, or these latter day contingent laws passed by men proficient in the new techniques of oratory, who were able to gain ascendancy over the many by securing for them the privileges and wealth that were once enjoyed only by the noble and able few? Instinctively, they would have said that he means the former; but they could see that, by his actions, it is the latter, the laws that guaranteed the Greeks their honor as free men and the aristocracy its greatness, that he is flouting and that Medea, the barbarian, is upholding as she defends her own and her children's honor. Paradoxically, she, not Jason, seems to be the one making the stand at Thermopylae and obeying the unwritten, divine law of oaths and the inviolability of an honorable

12. *Medea*, 545–46/537–38. The compression of the English version "Justice, not force, rules here." obscures this point, which is clear in the Greek: "You . . . are acquainted with justice and enjoy laws without having to gratify force (i.e., do favors to the powerful or submit to their will)."

man's word: "Whatever it commands [she does]; and its commandment is always the same: it ... requires [her] to stand firm, and either to conquer or die" (Herodotus, *Persian Wars* 7.104, tr. George Rawlinson). If along with Aegeus (cf. 690/695) the audience found themselves agreeing with Medea's stronger case—if they found themselves censuring Jason—they would logically be obliged to censure themselves, too.

But Jason in his argument with Medea does not stop with pointing out the benefits she has reaped by having the privilege of learning Greek laws and being lauded by Greek poets. He goes on to maintain how very advantageous, despite appearances, his new marriage arrangements are to Medea and her children, how they do not really represent the dissolving of an old friendship but its expansion. With Creon as a near connection by marriage and with future royal half brothers as kin, they will be so much safer, wealthier, and better placed politically than they would have been on their own. Truly, he had not acted out of lust; he had acted the way a savvy Greek vying for a place at the head of the table always acted, to satisfy ambition and the constraints of altered political circumstances. In other words, he makes a lame excuse to justify an arrangement that increased his own honor but destroyed Medea's.

Much that is strange in this play can be made more intelligible if we remember how crucial honor was to the calculations of all the Greeks. In our society nonconformity, independence, and self-reliance are prized, even in women. But this kind of individualism (a nineteenth-century word) is alien to the ancient world, not just in women, who were praised when compliant and invisible, but even in men, whose duty it was always to be striving to promote their honor and the honor of their family. The leadings of conscience meant nothing to them. Their very being, their selfhood was bound up in the opinion others had of them. In their small world of virulent family feuding, especially the privileged upper-class part of it, honor—the respect due to position and achievement, openly acknowledged every hour of every day—was everything. Breeding (high birth and the right education), wealth, talent, physical presence, offices won and successfully administered, above all prowess in war, both as a strategist and as a fighter in the front lines—these were the things that counted most, these and the fact that they were known to and approved of by others, especially one's peers and betters. "Fame," as Jason so pointedly observes (548/542–44), "is the important thing," for it was the measure of a man's greatness. Being top dog on a desert island or in faraway Colchis was tantamount to not being at all. A man who had lost his honor, whom no one feared or respected, had nothing left to fall back on, nothing to make life meaningful.

To such men as these, there was nothing more glorious to be sought than to die in battle, fighting for the city of one's fathers and the honor of one's house. The 300 Spartans who fell at Thermopylae against an overwhelmingly superior Persian force reached the pinnacle of honor and had for their reward lasting glory, because they had subordinated all their personal desires for the salvation of Greece and to uphold the honor of their ancestors. Conversely, to have survived the battle by some incalculable misfortune, like being behind the lines on sick leave, was a disgrace worse than dying unburied on a desert shore, for living in Sparta after Thermopylae meant enduring day after day the open contempt and open laughter of those who had once feared, respected, and praised you. You had gone from being a Somebody to being less than a Nobody, and there was no place to hide from this fact. "When Aristodemus [who had survived Thermopylae because he had been ill and unable to fight] returned to Lacedaemon [Sparta], reproach and disgrace awaited him; disgrace inasmuch as no Spartan would give him a light to kindle his fire, or so much as address a word to him; and reproach, since all spoke of him as the craven" (Herodotus, *Persian Wars* 7.231, tr. George Rawlinson).

In the honor game women too had a strategic part to play, and they knew it. Though subordinate, they were essential to their husbands and fathers, not just biologically as mothers of their children and grand-children, but as keepers of their own and their houses' reputations as well. How large a dowry and how much political influence they brought to their husbands' houses, how well they managed the house-hold staffs and the storerooms, how modestly they comported them-selves inside and outside the home, even how good they looked (for beauty adds grace to virtue and enlarges praise)—these things really mattered. But what mattered most, the thing that brought them the greatest personal honor, because by its means they proved themselves capable of bearing noble, purebred offspring, was their chastity—before marriage their virginity and after marriage the sanctity and purity and, indeed, the discreet privacy of the marriage bed.

In honor due a woman, as the Nurse tells us at the beginning of the play, Medea stood at the top, and her unmerited demotion from a proud and revered legitimate wife to the exposed, degraded position of a concubine had destroyed her honor as surely as illness had destroyed the honor of the Spartan Aristodemus, with this important exception: misfortune was not the cause of her disgrace; Jason was. She had never been at fault in their marriage, but he had treated her as though she had been, and, as far as she was concerned, he had done this for no good reason. If she had been barren or had crossed him in his public or private life, her fall would have been hard but understandable. As it was, he had acted just to aggrandize himself, to serve his own pleasure, for lust (as she saw it) and convenience and apparent, not true, honor. The Greeks had a good word for this kind of transgression, *hubris*: intentional and arrogant insult, any action that purposely depreciates or shows too little respect for another worthy of respect.

If the marriage of Jason and Medea had been in any way ordinary, his arrogant trampling underfoot of the just pride of a weak woman whose protector he was supposed to be would have been wrong but perhaps pardonable, since in the ancient honor code, his honor trumped hers. Regrettable as such divorces might be, they were sometimes necessary. The man, the stronger, ultimately determined the right. But as Euripides' audience well knew and as Medea herself reminds her women friends (**271 ff./251** ff.), theirs was no ordinary marriage. She had been no meek bride obedient to her father's will, but Jason's companion in arms, who had more than once given him tangible aid against his mortal enemies. Her reward for her help in his foreign and domestic wars had been her marriage. Under such circumstances their union could not be deemed a mere alliance between two families, but something more electric, a blood pact between fellow conspirators, who were honor bound to harm each other's enemies and do good to each other's friends.

In the computation and retention of honor, harming one's enemies was not just a duty, it was a coveted mark of success. By contrast, to hurt one's friends without cause, to disrespect them, was despicable. The trick lay in being able to distinguish between them, in order not to do the wrong things to or with the wrong people. Feelings, especially strong feelings, were better ignored or muted, for they could easily lead one astray, as they did Medea, whose passion for Jason had deluded her into thinking him a worthy ally. Of course, affection, even love, played a cementing role, especially among close friends, but in the ancient city, where no higher impersonal corporate authority as yet defined or provided for the common good, friendships were too important to be left to affection. They involved careful, reasoned deal making, for a friend was not necessarily someone you liked, but someone to whom you owed tangible benefits and who owed you benefits in return. Friendships not formed for pleasure's sake, though pleasure might indeed result, but for honor's, for visible political gain and prestige, were negotiated in many ways, marriage alliances being but one of them—albeit an extremely important one because they stood at the intersection of two basic kinds of friendships, those determined by blood and those based on agreement. Although marriage was, of course, intended to enlarge and perpetuate the former, in origin it belonged to the latter, those freely made, which were designed to advance family honor and the honor of the participants and their kin. When peacefully negotiated between responsible, rational parties—like Creon and Jason—they might indeed lead to unforeseen political calamities, especially if the contracting parties were leaders in their cities, but they were not calamitous in themselves, like the one Medea, *in loco patris*, forged with the desperate Jason.

Among voluntary friendships, the purest, most emotionally intense were not marriages, but those made by the young among their peers. The Greeks termed such friends *hetairoi*, that is, the friends of the shield or comrades with whom one marched in battle, engaged in politics, did business, formed a cult or even a cabal. Although they might include kin, and often did, kinship was incidental to their basic conception. Indeed, such friendships might even include former enemies. In large cities, just as the assembly was a meeting of the army and veterans, this model of comradeship defined many nonfamilial associations, the sworn alliances called *hetairiai*. Such friendships might be formed, for example, to forward a public concern or commercial enterprise. But sometimes they had the force of life and death alliances formed in times of extreme danger for the purpose of overthrowing a common enemy by force of arms. Of this latter kind was Medea's marriage pact, a joining of forces by two natural enemies under such duress that, like other life and death pacts, it was sealed by an oath, taken "over a [blood] sacrifice without blemish," whereby the two parties swore to "pray that he who observes this oath may be blessed abundantly: but that he who observes it not may perish from the earth, both he and his house."[13]

Thus, it was under constraints of this kind of oath that Medea avenged herself upon Jason to restore the honor his *hubris* had taken away. We can measure its putative binding power by the way in which the gods themselves fail to censure Medea's vengeance. To fulfill its terms and avoid the humiliation she might endure if she tried to attack Jason in person and failed, she made his life a living death and destroyed his house, rather than him, by slaughtering his new wife and

13. After a law of Solon, decreed by the democratic Assembly in 410, concerning slaying with impunity any enemy of the Athenians; quoted in Andocides's speech, "On the Mysteries," paragraphs 97–98, tr. K. J. Maidment (Loeb, 1941).

her own darling boys, the latter an act so terrible, so polluting to the Greeks that it required annual rites of expiation for all time to come (1353–57/1378–83) as compensation. Yet despite her palpable grief, she remains utterly unrepentant; nor is she punished for her crime. Instead she flies off to the temple of Hera and thence to Athens, in a conveyance provided by her ancestor, the Sun, the very god appointed to be the eye of the world's all-powerful enforcer and judge, Zeus. It is as if only the destruction of Jason's whole house, including his children (106–9/112–14), would satisfy the bloodthirsty Underworld avengers, set loose upon the earth by his breaking of the mighty wartime oath by which he had bound himself to this superhuman woman (163–66/160–63).

What we see at work here is a merciless, more primitive kind of justice, far removed from our abstract, carefully defined notions of law and order and closer to the kind of sublegal justice portrayed in *The Godfather*. Jason's sons' were necessary victims, whose death completed the punishment exacted by the Underworld; the annihilation of his house was guaranteed by the oath he had sworn and sealed by blood offerings poured into the earth and by the curses he had himself invoked. Although in this instance retribution was swift, it need not have been. Indeed, Jason himself, blindly trusting in the genuineness of his goodwill toward Medea and his own innocence — after all, under the pressure of circumstance he had done nothing more than other honor-seeking, realistic Athenians would have done with impunity — believes that the death of his boys must be delayed retaliation for the earlier death of Medea's brother back in Colchis (1306–7/1333). His line of reasoning was familiar to and accepted by many in Euripides' audience.

Although most in that audience would have readily acknowledged the power of animate blood and of the Underworld gods who drank it eventually to punish Jason for his wrongdoing, even by the killing of his sons, to judge by the Chorus, they would have found it difficult to justify Medea's making herself their instrument. While the compensation demanded by the gods for the violation of a powerful, sacred oath might explain the bloody outcome of the plot, it does not explain how Medea, who knew what she was doing—she was no "deranged housewife"—was able to force herself to commit what amounted to self-murder, the spilling of her own blood. Looked at from one perspective, the demonic, she was justified; from another, the ethical, she was not: hence the emphasis in the play upon her corrosive anger and how deeply she felt the insult of the blow Jason had dealt her. Repeatedly she expresses her horror at the derisive laughter of those she now considers her enemies (787–88/797), aimed not just against herself (1328–30/1354–57) but also against her children, if they were to remain in Jason's house (771–72/781–82, 1035–37/1059–61) or be buried by Jason (1353–55/1378–81). This horror of insult was something Euripides' audience with their explosive, Mafia-like contentiousness, would have understood, even if we do not. For them as for Medea, it was an irresistible motivating force. Medea had risked everything for Jason, not just the undying enmity and disgrace of her father's house but her own life and honor as well. Her reward was a marriage bed shared with Greece's greatest captain and the head of one of Greece's richest, most powerful, and lordly houses, to whose welfare she contributed unstintingly, for she was more than Jason's Mamma Corleone; she was his loyal, irreproachable *consigliere*. No wonder then that Jason's betrayal cut so deep. Euripides' audience would have understood the depths of Medea's uncontrollable anger, her dread of public shaming, and her thirst for the sweet honey of revenge. When wronged in the privileges of the marriage bed, even ordinary women become bloody minded (281–83/263–66). But would they have thought that Medea's fear of imagined future insults against her boys justified her, their nourisher and ally, in killing them? Drama with its many voices and diverse points of view shuns easy answers. But in this instance I think not, and not for sentimental reasons so much as for the fact that in killing them she had violated not just another unwritten law but one as strong as nature itself, the bond between mother and child.

Beyond the wildest imaginings of even the most callous Athenian, Medea had succeeded in wreaking total vengeance on her betrayer, but in so doing she had betrayed herself. In the grip of this palpable paradox, chances are that the audience, as they marveled at Medea rising in her chariot with the sun, sat in dumb silence, afraid not just for themselves and their own precarious honor—what man in that audience did not fear the power of women, especially able women they could not control, to undo them behind their backs—but for mankind's inability to fathom the Underworld's—and Zeus's—inexorable logic.

ON THE TRANSLATION

The story of Medea is one of the best known from ancient Greece and the play is one of the most widely translated Greek tragedies. As a result readers come to *Medea* knowing in some detail what will happen. Unlike other Greek tragedies there are no strong reversals and few surprises. When the play begins events have already reached a crisis. The Nurse tells us that Medea is starving "herself, except from grief/ and endless hours of crying/ . . . she loathes her children" (21–32). Medea, Jason, and their children are on a fast track to murder and destruction. There will be no veering. Added to this is the fact that for a modern reader or audience inured to the public flaunting of unhappy relationships between celebrities, Medea's sacrifice of her two sons to avenge Jason's divorce and remarriage is an act of such enormity that it seems excessive and unbelievable. All of this pushes the play in the direction of melodrama. One of my biggest concerns as a translator was to find a way to control the almost hysterical emotional energy of the play so that it avoided becoming shrill with anger and blame or claustrophobic with revenge. This is a problem that modern actors and directors can partially solve through setting, pacing, gesture, and tone. I wanted, however, to make the text itself capable of controlling and releasing this emotional energy so as not to exhaust the reader too soon as well as to make the tragic events more plausible. In the end, I wanted the play to read with the force and clarity of a dramatic poem.

Uncertain of how to solve the problem of melodrama, I began by tightening and compressing the language. I found that a fairly regular iambic rhythm might control the play's emotional urgency—somewhat—and that if the diction remained plain and direct, the characters might begin to speak in distinct ways. The range of diction I had in mind was that in Robert Frost's "A Servant to Servants," "The Death of the Hired Man," and other of his dramatic narratives. It is my hope that the meter and diction of the translation, along with the voice of the speakers rising from these elements, offer the reader and dramatist a version of *Medea* that approximates the tonal shifts and emotional tensions in Euripides's incomparable play.

A great part of the pleasure of working on this project has been in the collaboration with Georgia Machemer. Her line-by-line and often word-by-word translation guided me through the controversies and uncertainties that inhabit the original text. The suggestions and corrections she has given me have been invaluable as has been her support. David Kovacs's 1994 Loeb *Medea* provided an extremely useful starting point as did translations by Philip Vellacott, Frederic Raphael and Kenneth MacLeish, and John Harrison. Many discussions with Tom Sleigh, who had finished a translation of Euripides' *Herakles* as I was beginning *Medea*, helped to steady and encourage me.

Cornwall, Vermont MICHAEL COLLIER
February 2006

MEDEA

CHARACTERS

NURSE of Medea

TUTOR to Jason and Medea's children

MEDEA daughter of Aietes, King of Colchis

CHORUS of Corinthian women with their leader

CREON king of Corinth

JASON leader of the Argonauts

AEGEUS king of Athens

MESSENGER servant in Jason's household

CHILDREN Jason and Medea's two sons

Enter NURSE *from the house.*

NURSE If only the Argo had not tricked the sea,
had not flown on its wings past the Clashing Rocks
to Colchis! If only the pines of Mount Pelion
had not been hewn for the heroes' oars,
who rowed for Pelias to win the Golden Fleece!
Then my mistress Medea would not have sailed
to the walls of Iolcus, her heart broken
with love for Jason, or have persuaded the daughters
of Pelias to kill their father or be living now
in Corinth with her husband and children,   10
a refugee who's won respect, admired—stable,
domestic—supporting her husband as she should.

But now she hates all things. What love remains
is sick. Jason has left his sons and my mistress
for a royal bed and bride—the daughter
of Creon, the king who rules this land.
                              Medea,
enraged, recites the list of Jason's vows,
mocks the way he raised his hand as pledge
and demands the gods stand witness to what
her faithful love's produced.   20
Now she starves herself, except from grief
and endless hours of crying since she learned
her husband's wrongs.
                              She won't look up.
Her eyes fixed to the floor. She is deaf
to friends' advice, like a stone, like a wave.
The only thing she does is turn away
her lovely face to grieve in solitude—
her father, land and home—what she abandoned
to come here with the man who's now dishonored her.
Poor woman, misfortune's taught her what it means   30
to live without a country.

37

She loathes her children. They bring no pleasure
when she sees them. I'm afraid of what she's
thinking—fueled by her vengeful temper
to some new plot. She is dangerous.
I know how she responds to treachery.
No one who goes against her can win.
                                    But now
her sons return from play unaware of trouble.
Innocence protects itself from grief.

TUTOR   Old slave of my mistress' house, why are you   40
        alone outside the entrance, filling up
        your ears with your own complaints?
        Can Medea afford idleness like yours?

NURSE   Old tutor to Jason's sons, if servants
        are loyal, they take on their master's misfortune
        as if it were their own, deep and heartfelt.
        So great is my grief I've come outside
        to make the earth and sky listen to Medea's troubles.

TUTOR   And still she moans and grieves?

NURSE   What do you know? Her pain has just begun.   50
        Its pitch rising.

TUTOR   I shouldn't say this, but she's a fool
        and worse for what she doesn't know.

NURSE   What's that? What she doesn't know?

TUTOR   No, I was wrong to bring it up.

NURSE   Surely you can trust me with your secret.
        I'm a slave like you.

TUTOR   I was passing near the sacred water of Peirene,
        where old men throw dice, when I heard one of them
        mention Creon. I slowed down, pretending not
                to listen,   60

38

and overheard that the King would soon exile
  these children
and their mother. Drive them out of Corinth.
Don't ask if it's true. I don't know.

NURSE Jason will be a party to this? Exile his sons?
His argument is with Medea.

TUTOR That marriage is finished. He has a new wife.
He's no longer bound to honor Medea.

NURSE Doom follows evil and the sea rushes in
to fill a sinking boat.

TUTOR Why talk of doom. Hold your tongue.   70
Now is not the time to incite Medea more.

NURSE But children, now you know about your father.
I'd like to see him die! Yes, I would! But he's
  my master.
And yet his faithlessness is too awful, unheard of.

TUTOR That a man, a hero, abandons his wife and children,
bestows his love on someone new,
and at the same time keeps his self-regard—
  unheard of?
What world have you been living in?

NURSE That's enough!
          Children, go inside. I promise, nothing
          will happen.   80
And you, keep them from Medea.
When they are near, her eyes are fierce, savage like
  a bull
as if she'd trample them with anger.
When she breaks out, let's hope the children aren't
  around.
Let's hope her enemies receive this wrath instead.

MEDEA   *Sung from within.*

My hope is death!
Death's sorrow my gift!
My gift . . . my wretchedness!

NURSE Quickly! Didn't I predict this?
Your mother's fuming anger—   90
despair at its boil.
Hide from her.
Rage must not find its target.
She came into the world fierce
and stubborn and then she learned
to hate. Go inside,
don't look back!

                    Exit TUTOR *and* CHILDREN *into house.*

Her cries are nothing now.
But when she learns about her exile?
We'll see how the sky   100
catches fire. We'll see
how she feeds those flames
with her implacable hate.

MEDEA I suffer!
Nothing can answer it.

I want my children dead.
I want his house destroyed,
to crush my sons
and their father beneath it.

NURSE She'll make the children pay   110
for their father's treachery.
Reason and moderation is what's needed.
Time to think. What else can I do?
Her power makes her dangerous.
Privilege provides a license
for her violent moods. If she
were more like me, more like others,

that would tame her.
I aim for dignity in old age
to bring a modest honor   120
and enough money for my needs.
It's no good if your means
exceed your grasp.
The gods will notice
and then your fortune
pays for ruin.

                                    Enter CHORUS.

CHORUS I heard her voice. I heard
        the desolate cry of the Colchian.
        Her lamentation called me out
        from deep inside my house —   130
        a neighbor whom I befriended —
        and so the misfortunes
        of her house are mine.
        Nurse, what will soothe her?

NURSE How do you soothe utter desolation?
       How do you say, "Climb out
       from your abyss, reach up
       to your friends. They'll help
       you stand among the ruins
       of your home?
                        Oh, yes,   140
       and that man who's looking on,
       the one who married Creon's daughter?
       He used to be your husband."

MEDEA   Zeus's thunderbolts kill!
        Cleave my head!
            Peace will then
        spill out!

        That's a cure.

CHORUS Listen, Zeus, and Earth and the Light!
        She sings a dark destructive song.

Medea, why lie down with death?   150
Why let desire have fatal sway?
Death is always near.
Don't pray for it.
Don't kill yourself with grief.
Trust in Zeus. His justice
is the way to settle scores.
Grief is what the newly married Jason
feeds you. Spit it out!

MEDEA Before I betrayed my father,
before I butchered my brother at home   160
then dropped him from the Argo,
piece by piece, like bait,
I made Jason swear to love
and honor me, for after my shameful treason,
I thought only great oaths would keep
him bound to me.

Themis and Artemis, brave goddesses,
enforce those vows—or let me see Jason
and his princess buried
beneath the rubble of their house.   170

NURSE Do you hear her terrible prayers?
How she begs Themis and Zeus
the guardian of oaths
to revenge the broken vows?
All along I've feared she needs
cruelty to soothe her rage.

CHORUS Then, go, Nurse, tell Medea
we are outside, faithful friends,
women who can bear the worst
of what she feels.
                    When she sees us,   180
our voices will be a song
that calms her anger.
Do this quickly, no excuses.
Time is all she needs

to carry out cruel plans.
Who knows, her cries,
already come too late . . .

NURSE I'll go. I can't refuse orders.
I'll make duty the pleasure
that hides my fears.
              She'll growl   190
and snarl when I approach,
like a lioness shielding
her cubs. She'll snort like a bull.
I doubt I'll lure her out.
But I'll go.

        NURSE *starts to leave, then turns back to* CHORUS.

I know a servant shouldn't talk
like this, but your singing voices
won't heal Medea.
When men invented song,
they had in mind decoration
for festivals and banquets,   200
pretty tunes.
Think how much better off
we would be if music
like a magic spell could reverse
the bitter histories of our lives
or cure human sorrow.
As it is I wouldn't bother
with the twanging lyre,
let the gorged and drunken
fall asleep happily   210
in their cups
that's enough satisfaction . . .

CHORUS Again we hear the lamentations,
her fury rehearsing
Jason's grotesque betrayal.
Again she invokes Themis's help,
the goddess of oaths,
who guided Medea

over the haunted sea
and through the impassable maw   220
that guards the way to Greece.

MEDEA Women of Corinth, here I am, as you wish
and not as you might think, uncaring.
                             All of us
know women who no matter the occasion
remain decorous, or because they stay at home
are thought to be cold and implacable,
indifferent to their neighbors' needs.
All of us judge by sight and not by knowledge.
Because I'm an outsider I know this better than most,
and have worked hard to fit in,   230
but not, like some, I hope,
in a prideful or aggressive way—
even so I'm a target of suspicion,
especially since Jason, yes, my faithless husband,
tore out the threads I'd stitched to hold
our life together. So quickly and suddenly
was it done, I wasn't given time to console
myself or build alliances with friends.
A brutal man whom I once loved has smashed me
in the face so hard I wear the face of death.   240

What other creatures are bred so exquisitely
and purposefully for mistreatment as women are?
Think of how we buy ourselves husbands,
power and alliances for them, slavery
and conquest over us. Bad enough
to have no choice in servitude—
but to pay for it and then celebrate
a wedding feast adds salt to the wound.
Try refusing the arrangement, or later
petition for divorce—the first is impossible   250
while the second is like admitting
you're a whore.
                             And who ever warned us
of a husband's rough hands,
breath aflame on our neck, or the inscrutable

customs of his house?
Some of you will say, "It's not
that bad"; and with work can learn the rules
and maybe find a meager happiness.
But as hard as we try to do the pleasing thing,
it usually leads to resentment, 260
complaints about our moods.
That's why when they seek out friends
for entertainment, death looks so good to us,
much better than our husbands who think
we adore only them, grateful that they,
not us, go off to war. But they're wrong!
deluded by soldier fantasies.
If they like pain and danger let them take
a turn at bearing children and for every birth
I'll fight three wars. 270

But I've been talking as if our lives
are the same. They're not. You are Corinthians
with ancestral homes, childhood friends,
while I, stripped of that already,
am now even more exposed by Jason's cruelties.
Remember how I came here, a war bride,
plundered from my country, an orphan?
Now who's obligated to shelter me? Not you,
I know. As you watch my plans for justice unfold,
keep them secret, that's all I ask. I've never felt 280
this threatened nor fearless: men win their battles
on the field but women are ruthless when the bed
becomes the battleground. We've lain
in our own blood before . . . and have survived.

CHORUS Medea, now I understand your grief
and why your husband's treachery
must be revenged. Go ahead, I won't tell.

Enter CREON.

But, look, our king approaches.
He's come to listen and advise.

CREON I've decreed your immediate exile   290
       from Corinth, Medea. This includes
       your children. Get your things together.
       An escort's waiting to take you to the border.
       Hurry up!
       Later you can twist your face like that
       and rage against your husband all you want.

MEDEA You, too, will drown me in the storm
       unleashed by my husband?
       Did he send you to cut away the sails,
       and clear the decks of my last hope?   300
       If not, then why this "Hurry Up!,"
       this unseemly rush to exile?

CREON The truth is I fear you'll harm my daughter.
       Why? Because your nature, clever and vindictive,
       thrives on evil and because you sting with loss.

       A king has many ears,
       through them he hears the darkest threats
       made against his house.
       I've heard yours.
       I know about your plans, so why should I wait?
       Exiling you now is my best protection.   310
       If I let you stay, a woman like you
       will only hate me more for my weakness.

MEDEA A woman like me! What am I like
       that's different from you or any man,
       except I'm a woman who is clever . . .
       and that's my reputation? Then no one,
       man or woman, should be encouraged
       to be clever. Stay dumb!
       It's easier to fit in with fools.
       Fools, educated or not, will resent   320
       you for what you know. A woman like me
       is mistrusted and despised for her cleverness,
       feared by you because your fear's misplaced.
       Creon, I'm not so clever. Don't fear me.

I haven't the power to kill a king.
Besides what harm have you done me?
Like any father you arranged your daughter's
marriage to make the best match.
I respect that.
                    It's my husband I hate.
Yet I wish your alliance well.   330
From now on I'll be quiet about my wrongs
and respect the judgment of my betters.
That's difficult for me to say. All I want
is for you to let us stay in Corinth!

CREON You'd do better persuading me
with a fit of rage. A woman like you
keeps planning harm no matter
what she says. Meekness
is more dangerous than guile. Even if you
silenced your hate I would never believe it.   340
I won't be tricked by an enemy.
Exile is what I've decreed.
Immediate! Irrevocable!

MEDEA A woman like me never begs. But look . . .
I beg you.

CREON So don't try. You can't convince me.

MEDEA But you are bound by my plea to listen.

CREON No: I'm bound to protect my family and home first.

MEDEA I need my birthplace more than ever now.

CREON I love my children first and then my home.

MEDEA Yes, but what we love too much is dangerous.   350

CREON That depends, sometimes it's dangerous not to love.

MEDEA Zeus, you won't forget who caused our pain.

CREON Go, the longer you stay the more trouble you bring.

MEDEA No: my trouble starts when I go.

CREON If you don't go, my men will throw you out.

MEDEA Creon, I told you I never beg, but look I'm begging!

CREON I don't call this begging! You're defying my decree!

MEDEA No, I accept exile.

CREON Then let go of my hand, stand up!
　　　What do you want?   360

MEDEA A day's reprieve to prepare for exile
　　　gracefully. And since my husband loves
　　　his new home more than his children
　　　I need to plan their future carefully.
　　　Put yourself in my place. You'll feel differently.
　　　As a father you can see the children
　　　aren't to blame. Exile is not new to me,
　　　but it will crush my sons.

CREON I'm not a rigid tyrant. Mercy
　　　has undermined my resolve before.   370
　　　I'll regret my wavering. Nevertheless
　　　you can have one day on one condition:
　　　When the sun comes up tomorrow
　　　if you and your children have not crossed
　　　the border, you die.
　　　Stay if you must.
　　　One day won't give you time
　　　to work the wicked plans I fear. Ask no more.   377

                                        Exit CREON.

CHORUS Medea, you're doomed!
　　　An exile needs help and protection,
　　　a destination and shelter.   380

48

Where will you go?
To whom will you turn?

MEDEA   You're right! My situation's bad,
exile's made it dire but don't think
there isn't time to settle the score
with the newlyweds and their procurer.
When I kissed Creon's leprous hands,
when I got on my knees and begged,
it was not for pity but for a brief reprieve.
If he had stood his ground I'd have no hope,   390
but foolish as he is, now I have a day,
and a day is long enough to make of him,
his daughter, and the one I used to love
a heap of bones.

So, friends, what method should we use?
Hard to choose. I could torch them
in their love nest or butcher them sleeping
in their fragrant bed. These require stealth,
luck more than nerve and style.
Nothing could be worse if I were caught   400
lurking in their house. They'd mock and laugh
at me intolerably before putting me to death.
Better to reach them directly without detection.
I'll do what I do best. I'll poison them.

See how easy it is to kill!
But when they're dead where will I go?
What country or household will welcome
and protect me? None.
If someone should arrive to rescue me,
though time is short, then I'll use silence   410
and trickery to carry out the murder,
but if no protector comes then I'll attack
directly with an unmistakable sword
and die along with those I kill.

Hecate, dearest of my household gods,
by your dark magic I will repay

the pain and ridicule I've suffered.
Bitter with grief will be their marriage.
Bitter will be what Creon tastes
for his part in this alliance.   420
Bitter for me my banishment.

Come, I must be Medea, Hecate's servant,
artist of potions and spells of guile.
Listen to the voice of her suffering.
Hear what others hear, that Jason's
absurd marriage was made by outwitting you,
daughter of a king, granddaughter of the Sun!
Remember, you're a woman and it's useless
to compete with men like Jason.
Speak courage to yourself!   430
Be Medea, invent their grotesque murders.

CHORUS   Now sacred waters flow uphill
and the world where men
once honored oaths is parched.
Look, at last, women embody truth!

No longer will the ancient songs
that sing our faithlessness be sung.
If Apollo allowed us to carry a tune,
we'd write the epic of men's worst frailties.

We'd sing, Medea, of your inspired love,   440
how it guided you through the Black Sea.
We'd sing of what you lost, your fatherland,
a husband's love, and now your children's home.

The spell of trust is broken, and shame,
like you, is banished. Past and future hold
no welcome, while the present is a princess—
younger, stronger—who sleeps where you once slept.

                                   Enter JASON.

JASON Even before I met you, I knew rage
and anger were their own worst enemies.
Generous terms were offered you: the house,   450
protection, and privileges, but could you bear
these gifts without complaint? Now exile
is your reward. Keep railing at me.
Call me vile and disgusting. It doesn't matter.
But keep it up about Creon and his family
and exile will be a kindness.
And just so you know—I've been your advocate
with him because I wanted you to stay.
But could you stop your rant against the king?
You've bought your exile with your foolish mouth.   460

Still, after all the trouble you've caused
I won't be accused of neglect. I'm here
to do the right thing, to insure the children
and you have the means and money to endure
the worst exile will bring. For this I'm sure
you'll hate me, but it's a hate I won't return.

MEDEA How can I say what you are! Curses
won't answer your vileness and names
don't exist for your cowardice. In fact,
I doubt you're real. What real man,   470
so offensive to everyone, would think it
courageous to face the family
he's betrayed, and lie to them again?
But I'm glad you're here. I'll catalog your sins
and feel better for it while you feel worse.

I'll start at the beginning, and if you don't
remember, ask any Argonaut—they
saw how I saved your life when my father
challenged you to harness the fire-breathing bulls,
plough the field of death, and sow the monster seeds.   480
I killed the insomniac serpent coiled
inseparably around the Golden Fleece,
whose light and shimmer raised by me
brought your success instead of death.

More eager than wise, I abandoned
my country and father to follow you
to Iolcus where I engineered your uncle's
murder, wasting that house, too, with grief
and death. All this I did for you!
And in return you honored me   490
with contempt, betrayal, a replacement wife.
I might understand your disappointment
if I'd been barren but I gave you sons!

Now your promises are worthless.
Or have the gods allowed you
to make new rules that govern oaths?
See my right hand, how often you spoke
in pledge to it, how often you bowed
your head—an earnest supplicant.
You lied then as you lie now,   500
a thief of all my better hopes.

Come then, if you want, I'll speak to you
as a friend and ask the questions a friend
would ask. And when you can't respond,
I'll have shown what kind of friend you are.
So, as an exile where should I go? Home
to my father whom I betrayed for you?
To the cousins who stewed your uncle
with my recipe? I'm sure they'd set
an extra place so I could eat with them.   510
That's how things stand, friend.
For you, I became my family's worst enemy.
For you, I set my fatal traps
and in return you made a spectacle of me
for all of Greece to see. What do they imagine
as I'm sent from my home, alone, except
with the children you've abandoned? That Jason
is a faithful, honest husband? Surely
your new wife is reassured to see
your sons poor and homeless, and me—   520
the *former* wife—who betrayed herself
to save you, destroyed again.

Why has Zeus given us the alchemy
that detects true gold from false
and yet withheld the means
to expose evil in men?

CHORUS Stronger than lover's love is lover's hate
Incurable, in each, the wounds they make.

JASON I suppose I should stand here
and ride out the tiresome storm   530
of your complaint, put on my captain's hat,
reef sail, and drag anchor to your mood.
But I can't bear how you exaggerate
your selfless role in my success.
I know how I was saved. Powerful Aphrodite!
She led me to the Golden Fleece and back.
And you, yes, you have a mind for plots
and treachery, but Cupid had to wound you
with his darts before you moved. Go ahead,
remind me I'm ungrateful.
                                   I won't say   540
your passion wasn't real. I won't say
you didn't help, you did. And for it
you've been paid more than you deserve. Listen,
and I'll prove it.
                        Now, you live in Greece—
the center of the world. Justice, not force,
rules here. Here your cleverness has brought you
fame. Out beyond the Black Sea, no one sings
in praise of you.
                        To me, fame is the important thing.
I'd give up all I owned for it.
What good is a voice like Orpheus's   550
if no one knows it belongs to you?
Remember who started this war of words.
That's all I'll say to counter your account.

As for my royal marriage, if your reproaches
weren't so blind, you'd see it as a plan—

ingenious, disciplined, farsighted —
to support you and the children.

MEDEA: *furious.*

If you'd just listen, for once, maybe you'd
remember we fled Iolcus and washed up here,
broken refugees. So what better reversal   560
than to marry the daughter of a king?
      That I
grew bored with you in bed and wanted
a younger wife? These thoughts drive your anger.
Or that I want to father more sons?
The ones I have — yours and mine —
are more than adequate.
       I remarried
so we might prosper and live in the comfort
we deserve, surrounded by true friends.
If I should have more sons, they'll be
brothers to ours, not rivals.   570
I've forged an alliance that protects
and elevates us all. Children are more important
to fathers than to mothers. My unborn sons
will save our living ones.
      Is this plan bad?
No, you'd admire what I've done if sex
wasn't your obsession.
      It's folly
that women measure their happiness
with the pleasures of the bed, but they do.
And when the pleasure cools or their man goes
  missing,
all they once lived for turns dark and hateful.   580
If I could remake the world, I'd banish women,
send them away with all their trouble.
Then children would come from a purer source.

CHORUS Jason, reasonable words make reasonable arguments
    and I could believe them but truth lies in deeds
    and, I'm sorry to say, you left Medea.

MEDEA   A reasonable argument? Am I the only one alive
        who hears lies made reasonable by this liar?
        Shouldn't truth twisters be punished
        instead of listened to? Not, apparently, if they deceive   590
        as brazenly as Jason does. Where will he stop?
        But he's not so clever. Watch how my words
        will pin him to the mat.
                                If this marriage
        was part of such a selfless scheme, why hide it
        until now? Why not ask me for help?

JASON   Help? If I'd mentioned marriage, divulged my plan,
        what part of your hateful, broken heart
        would have come to my assistance?

MEDEA   The part that knows your shame to live
        the rest of your days with a barbarian like me   600
        was greater than your honor.

JASON   I'll say this one more time! I didn't need
        another woman. The marriage was strategic,
        a defensive ploy to protect you—to give our sons
        brothers connected to the throne.

MEDEA   I don't need fortune's gifts if they're made from pain
        or wealth derived from the heart's torture.

JASON   Wake up, Medea! Good fortune isn't painful.
        Be thankful for the chance to prosper.

MEDEA   Don't mock me! Fortune sends me wounded   610
        into exile, while the palace is your home.

JASON   Exile was your choice, don't blame fortune.

MEDEA   My choice? Did I abandon you?

JASON   No, you chose to curse the king.

MEDEA   Of course I did, just as I curse you.

JASON   I won't argue with you any longer.
My offer of help stands: money to ease
exile for the children and you. Also,
I have friends who can arrange to take you in.
Say the word. What's mine is yours.   620
It does no good to harden yourself
to charity. Leave behind your destructive anger.

MEDEA   I won't take help from you. Besides, your friends
are now my enemies and gifts from
a faithless man like you are bribes.

JASON   Then let the gods judge me. They see
my plan for you and the children is good.
They see this obstinate refusal of my help.
Remember, the gods can still make life worse for you.

MEDEA   Leave me, your impatience stinks of lust   630
for the new bride. Go and be the groom!
But listen well, your skill at marrying
will bring you a dowry of tears.

                                          Exit JASON.

CHORUS   See, how strong love overwhelms us.
See, how it wounds and destroys
and yet when Aphrodite wants to soothe,
nothing cures as love cures.
So, my love, shoot me gently,
barely break my skin with your terrible arrows.

Then I'll know happiness in life.   640
Then Aphrodite's urgings will enflame
my heart, but love will keep me faithful, far
from the wildness of a stranger's bed.
Then I'll know that when she chooses lovers,
it means that love will never fail.

O, and this sweet city, Corinth,
may I never be its poor exile.

May I never wander in realms
where pity is my name. Kill me
first, spare me life's worst torment   650
to lose your true home and native land.

This is no invented grief.
In Medea I have seen
the friendless suffering exile breeds.
Let those who promise love
and then defile it, die unloved
and never ask to be my friend.

Enter AEGEUS *in traveling clothes.*

AEGEUS Medea, greetings, happiness!
        What better hopes can friends express.

MEDEA Happiness to you Aegeus. Welcome.   660
       What brings you to Corinth?

AEGEUS I come from Delphi—Apollo's oracle.

MEDEA The world's most potent seer. Why?

AEGEUS To ask how I might father a child.

MEDEA Childless? How can that be?

AEGEUS I think by a god's curse.

MEDEA Are you married? Do you have a wife?

AEGEUS Yes and we find pleasure in our bed.

MEDEA What advice did Apollo have?

AEGEUS A riddle to confuse the most clever.   670

MEDEA Can you say it? Or have you been forbidden?

AEGEUS No, it begs for cleverness like yours.

MEDEA Then tell me. Don't hold back.

AEGEUS "Choke off the wineskin's spout," he warned.

MEDEA What else? For how long?

AEGEUS Until my journey ends at home.

MEDEA Yet by sailing here you're far from home.

AEGEUS I've come to speak with Pittheus, the Troezen king.

MEDEA Pelops's son, he's known for piety and wisdom.

AEGEUS I'll tell him what the oracle declared.   680

MEDEA He's nimble enough to solve the riddle.

AEGEUS And there's no better friend. A brave man in
          the ranks.

MEDEA Good luck and may you obtain all you desire.

AEGEUS But, Medea, I see your face is etched by tears.
                                        Why?

MEDEA Aegeus, my husband is vile. There's no one worse.

AEGEUS How? Tell me what darkness haunts you.

MEDEA It's his fault. He's wronged me. I'm blameless.

AEGEUS Fault? Blame? There's more, I can tell. Go on.

MEDEA He's thrown me out. Installed a new wife.

AEGEUS What's compelled him to act so shamelessly?   690

MEDEA His promises are lies. His love false.

AEGEUS Perhaps he's confused a brief passion for love.

MEDEA His passion is for faithlessness . . .

AEGEUS Then it's your duty to forget him.

MEDEA . . . and ambition. He's married the king's daughter.

AEGEUS What king consents to this?

MEDEA The Corinthian, Creon, who rules this land.

AEGEUS I understand your torment.

MEDEA And my exile? I've been sent away to die.

AEGEUS By whom? I see how trouble overwhelms you.   700

MEDEA Creon. My sentence starts tomorrow.

AEGEUS Where's Jason? He won't allow this.

MEDEA He acts appalled but won't do anything to help.

MEDEA *kneels before* AEGEUS *in supplication.*

By all that's honorable and wise in you,
you who recognize the shameful wrongs
I've endured, save me from friendless exile.
I need refuge in your country, protection in your
        home.
Do this and the gods may give you children.
Help me and you'll die a happy death.
Seize this moment that fortune brings.   710
I know recipes and spells to quicken men.
Let Medea end your quest for children.

AEGEUS Noble Medea, I'm ready to help.
I know the gods want justice.
I trust your magic will produce my sons.
Already I feel the burden lifting.

Listen and I'll lay out our plan:
The Corinthians honor me as their guest.
I won't insult them by stealing you away.
Instead you must reach Athens on your own.   720
There you'll be my guest. Do this
and Creon can't come demanding
that I give you up. My home will be
your best protection. I promise.

MEDEA I understand these obligations. Now restate your
            promise
as an oath. Only then will I feel secure.

AEGEUS Is it the plan or me you don't trust?

MEDEA Aegeus, you I trust but not my many enemies:
Pelias's sons, Creon . . .
                        An oath
Will keep your promises safe against   730
their powerful inducements to give me up.
I'm weak and need the gods to help.

AEGEUS Your argument, wise and measured,
is convincing. An oath provides me cover
from my enemies and gives you peace of mind.
Tell me which gods to swear by. I'll do it.

MEDEA Start with Gaia, then Helios, my grandfather,
and as usual, all the gods no matter where they be.

AEGEUS Yes, but what am I obliged to do? You've left that out.

MEDEA Swear never to exile me from Athens.   740
Never, on your life, no matter what they say,
agree to my enemies' demands to hand me over.

AEGEUS Gaia, Helios, and all the gods,
        I swear by Medea's spoken oath.

MEDEA   Exactly. And if you break this pledge?

AEGEUS May the gods punish me like others who renounce
        them.

MEDEA   Dear friend, go now, you have your happiness.
        Mine follows once I've carried out my plans.
        Then I'll come to Athens.

                                        Exit AEGEUS.

CHORUS LEADER May Hermes, protector of travelers,   750
        lead you safely home
        and may your eager wish for children
        be granted. Aegeus, a noble heart
        like yours deserves reward.

MEDEA   Zeus, your justice shines brightly under
        Helios's light. Look into that light, my friends,
        and you'll see victory lies ahead. What else
        could Aegeus's sudden appearance mean—
        his offer of safe harbor, but certain punishment
        for my enemies. Yes, and afterwards,   760
        I'll ride out the storm my vengeance has caused,
        securely docked in Athens.

        Listen, now it's time to unfold my plans,
        though what I say is certain to displease.

        I'll send a servant to summon Jason
        and when he comes, I'll tell him
        what he wants to hear: yes, his marriage,
        my abandonment—two parts of a brilliant plan.

        And since this concerns the children's fate,
        not mine, I'll suggest they remain with him.   770

But don't think for a moment I'd leave my sons
in this unfriendly land, targets for my enemies.

        No,
                the children are the bait I'll use to trap
and kill the princess bride.
Each will bear a gift to her —
one a priceless gown,
the other a diadem of supple gold.
She needs only to unwrap and touch
the precious things to die painfully,
and any one who touches her
infected corpse will die as well.   780

That's the easy part, all thought out
and what follows is more than unspeakable.
I must kill my children.
Only their deaths will bring down Jason's house.
Quickly I'll go into exile, guilty
forever of my sons' ungodly murders.
But this is easier to bear than my enemies
who mock me. Why should I care anymore?
And what's the good of living?
                        I can't restore   790
my home and country, no spell will release
misfortune's hold. I was wrong to leave
my father, wrong to let a Greek
seduce me with his promises.
But the gods will assist me. Jason
will pay for mistreating me.
                        The next time
he sees his sons, he'll see them dead
and his hideous bride — meant to bear
new sons — destroyed by my fatal potions.
Who then will dare to say I'm weak or timid?   800
No, they'll say I'm loyal as a friend, ruthless
as a foe, so much like a hero destined for glory.

CHORUS LEADER We've listened to you. We want to help.
               But the laws of man demand we urge you
               not to carry out your plan.

MEDEA The plan is set. Advice like yours lacks nerve
       and my experience with grief and suffering.

CHORUS LEADER Suffering so great you'll kill your sons?

MEDEA Yes, anything to make Jason's suffering worse than
       mine.

CHORUS LEADER And turn your grief into wretchedness and misery?   810

MEDEA Who can say? The time for talk has ended.

                                        To the NURSE.

       Go, find Jason. Invite him here.
       There's no one else I'd trust with this mission.
       If you are a woman truly loyal to me,
       you'll tell him nothing of my plans.

                                        Exit NURSE.

CHORUS Children of the gods, of sacred Earth,
        since ancient times, Athenians
        have flourished, unconquered, nourished
        by the vivid air that brings them
        grace and wisdom, a residue   820
        from when the muses once combined
        to fashion Harmony, their perfect child.

        A time, we're told, when Aphrodite
        drinking from the sweet Cephisus
        would fill the river valley with her breath,
        fragrant as roses that bind her hair,
        a scent that guides her Loves to wit,
        where side by side they invent
        beauty and excellence in every art.

How then can Athens   830
with its sacred river,
its land where gods find refuge
admit a murderer, fouled
by her children's slaughter,
to live among its citizens?
Consider the knife, the innocent throats,
the slit and cry and blood!
By all we know, we beg and plead:
Do not kill your sons!

And at that terrible moment   840
how do you know your heart
won't fail, hand not tremble
when you see the blade flash
in your children's eyes?
When it's your own sons
begging for their lives
then not even you—cold
hearted—will drench your hand
in their warm blood.

Enter JASON *accompanied by the* NURSE.

JASON As you command, I'm here, once more,   850
        ready to listen, though your enmity for me
        is clear . . .
                    Tell me, what's your new demand?

MEDEA I want, Jason, your forgiveness for all
        I've said, to understand that my anger
        is the other side of love provoked
        by years of happy marriage.
                        I've taken stock,
        talked to myself—and it's stubbornness,
        fed by rage, that blinds me to these preparations.
        Why should I oppose you and Corinth?
        You've conspired to make me more secure,   860
        to give our sons princes for brothers.
        Why not trade anger for peace? Give up suffering

and recognize the gods offer hope.
The truth is, the boys and I are exiles. We need
        friends.
I've come to realize calmness and steadiness
are what's required, a partner in your plan,
a proud bridesmaid to the nuptial
you've generously devised.

Women are not dumb and wicked by nature
but we are what we are. Knowing this,   870
you should avoid treating me the way
I treated you, answering a fool with foolishness.
Now that I've brought myself to this understanding
I can admit how wrong I was. Clear thinking
is all I needed to join your undertaking.

Children, come out, it's safe! Greet your father.
Speak to him with love. Our feud is over.
We've called a truce. Our hate has vanished.
Grip his right hand like men . . .
                        Now the future
lies ahead, its troubles hidden
                        . . . Children,   880
promise all life long you'll embrace me too.
Here's wretchedness, fear, foreboding, sorrow
I can't hold back. The quarrel with your father
made up and yet I'm moved to tears.

CHORUS LEADER My eyes, too, are soft from crying.
Let misfortune stop here where these tears fall.

JASON Good, you've got the right attitude now.
I'll let pass the earlier tantrums.
Women aren't made to share their husbands.
And though it took awhile for you to change   890
your mind about my triumphant plan . . .
Well, I'm glad that reason has returned.

My sons, your father's careful deliberations,
blessed by the gods, guarantee a better life

for you. Someday with your future brothers
you'll help to govern Corinth. Only now,
grow into men. Let your father
and a favoring god fashion your destiny.
Once you've reached your prime — strong,
    irrepressible —
I'll watch with satisfaction as you crush my enemies.   900

                  MEDEA *turns away from the scene weeping.*

Why keep crying? Why the downcast face?
Have my words again disturbed you?

MEDEA I'm fine. My concern is for the children.

JASON Why prolong this torture with your fears for them?

MEDEA I'm their mother! And when you begin to speak
about their futures, doubt and pity rush in.

JASON Their futures are safe, sealed. Give up your worries!

MEDEA Then I'll submit to what you say. Remember,
as a woman my nature is to cry.

But there are other reasons I summoned you: 910
I won't escape the king's decree of exile.
It's better that I'm banished. I'd be a hindrance
if I stayed, a source of suspicion
for all the threats I've made against his house.
I've reconciled myself to leaving Corinth,
and the children. In order for your plan
to work, you must raise the boys here.
Go, beg Creon not to send them into exile.

JASON He's stubborn and resolute, but I'll try.

MEDEA Start with your wife. Use her to persuade   920
her father the boys don't deserve banishment.

JASON Yes, with her I'll have success.

MEDEA That's right, if she's like other women,
       but let me help. I have a plan to send
       the children to her with gifts more beautiful
       than mortals know: a seamless gown,
       a diadem of supple gold . . .

                              To the SERVANTS.

                              Quickly,
       one of you go bring the treasures here.

                              To JASON.

       Look how fortune multiplies for her:
       first, a brilliant husband fills her bed   930
       and now these adornments, heirlooms that Helios,
       my grandfather, bequeathed to his descendants.

                    The SERVANT *returns with the gifts.*

       Boys, take these presents, hold them tightly,
       hand them to her highness, your father's radiant bride.
       Gifts like these she will more than embrace.

JASON Medea, this is foolish. Keep them for yourself.
       The palace has chests filled with fine garments,
       vaults of gold. Don't give up your legacy.
       If I have any say with my wife, my words
       will persuade more than your family's wealth.   940

MEDEA Don't count on it! Even gods like gifts.
       And men always prefer gold to promises.
       Her youth and status appeal to the gods,
       so let's treat her like a goddess. Gold, yes,
       but I'd give a life to buy the children freedom.

       Now, boys, go to the king's magnificent palace,
       get on your knees and beg your father's new wife,

my mistress, to stop your exile. Give her
these rare gifts. Most importantly, put them
only in her hands. Go quickly. Good luck.   950
I'll wait for your return and the news
that all your mother wishes for is true.

> Exit JASON *and* CHILDREN, *accompanied*
> *by the* TUTOR *and the* NURSE.

CHORUS Abandon hope that the children will survive.
Now they walk the murderous road.
The bride will embrace the lacework of gold,
blind to its enchanting ruin.
She will lace her beautiful hair
with death's poisonous ribbon.
Heavenly charms, Helios's crown of gold
and shimmering gown, glamour   960
she can't resist, though it makes her
a bride of the dead. The snare is set.
Death waits at the center.
No power can come to her rescue.

And you, unfortunate bridegroom
who engineered a royal marriage
to shape his destiny, could you have guessed
your plan would murder your sons
and deliver your bride to a hideous death?
Unlucky man, could you have been more wrong?   970

And Medea, you're wrong too,
in every way, sad and sadder still,
you'll kill your sons, justice too harsh
for Jason's heartless crimes—
your husband who left your marriage bed
to occupy another.

> *Enter* TUTOR *with the* CHILDREN.

TUTOR My lady, the princess took the gifts into her hands
and happily consented to give your sons reprieve.
In the House of Corinth they'll find happiness.

Medea turns away and weeps.

But why should good fortune make you sad?   980
Why turn away from my report?
Have I displeased you?

MEDEA Sadness everywhere!

TUTOR But the children are happy.

MEDEA Sadness is everywhere!

TUTOR I thought my news was good.
Tell me what I've said to upset you.

MEDEA You saw what you saw. You're not to blame.

TUTOR Then why the dark face and tears?

MEDEA Grief is all that's left. My vengeful schemes   990
and the gods' help have made it so.

TUTOR Think of the day your sons will bring you home!

MEDEA But first there are others I must carry home.

TUTOR Women lose their children frequently
so bear this sorrow as best you can.

MEDEA Yes, in time I will. But now go inside.
Get ready for the children's day. They'll follow soon.

Exit TUTOR *into the house.*

Children, my dear sons, this is your city.
Here is your home where you will start new lives,
bereft of me, your abandoned mother.   1000
I must begin my exile in a land
far from you, without the happiness
of seeing you grow and prosper, unable

to perfume your nuptial baths, arrange
the bridal sheets or light the wedding torches.
My unforgiving self has made me wretched.
And all I've done to raise you, the ceaseless work,
the excruciating pain of childbirth—
all count for nothing.

                      Foolishly I hoped
you'd care for me in my old age, dress my body   1010
when I died. What better fortune than to have
such sons.

                  But this sweet dream of life
has ended. Bereft of you I'll spend my days
in heart-broken grief. And you no longer
within sight of me will grow accustomed
to my absence.

Oh, children, I don't understand your looks.
Why smile as if it were your last?
I despair of what to do.

                     See, my strength
and resolve vanish in the children's   1020
lively faces. It can't be done.
Farewell to my schemes. When I leave, I'll take
my sons with me. Why should I make them
suffer to revenge their father and make
my own suffering so much worse? No, farewell.

And yet what will change? My foes
unpunished mock me.
Should I endure it? The pledges I've made
my heart have weakened me.

        The CHILDREN *begin to move toward the house.*

                    Boys, go into the house.
Now, only the sacred and pure are allowed   1030
to witness this sacrifice. My hand has strengthened.
Yet, my angry heart resists these urges.

Release the children. Spare them from my
    wretchedness.
In Athens they will bring me happiness.

But it's too late. By all of Hell's vengeful
demons I'll not leave my sons
for my enemies to ridicule.
               The children
must die. I gave them life and now
I'll take it. No more wavering. It's settled.
There, I see the princess wearing the crown   1040
and know the poisonous robe eats her flesh.
The path before me is filled with grief
but it's nothing like the dark road I'll send
my sons down.
             Let me say goodbye to them.

The CHILDREN *return to* MEDEA.

Children, give me your hands to kiss.
Sweet hands, sweet lips. Strong bodies
and noble faces. May happiness follow you
into that other place. Here your father
has stolen your happiness.
             Such tenderness,
my hand caressing your skin, your sweet breath —   1050
My sons.
            Leave me, go into the house.
I can bear no longer to look at you.
The horror of my evil overwhelms me.
Horror of what I'll do. Angry passions
have mastered me — emotions of misrule
that destroy men.

Exit the CHILDREN *into the house followed by* MEDEA.

CHORUS LEADER Many times I've joined in formal arguments
with men whose skill in the subtle art
of rhetoric was greater than my own
and lost. But all women aren't strangers   1060

to Wisdom's muse. Sometimes one of us
is chosen to be guided by the inspiring daughters.
And so my thoughts have led me to believe
that childless men and women lead lives
more fortunate than those with sons and daughters.
Although they never know the joy and pain
that children bring, they avoid
a much greater sum of trouble.
Households filled with children
are slaves to the work and worry of their care.   1070
The first concern is how to raise them,
then how they'll manage once they're grown.
Yet even when they're independent,
it's still uncertain if their success
will honor you for all you've done. But heartbreak
worse than what's produced by all these
common dangers lurks and waits.
Let's say the children turn out perfect.
Does fate care if fate has other plans?
Death comes to drag our children   1080
off to the underworld no matter how beloved.
You'd think the gods might offer inducements
to men and women for bothering to bring
children into the world; instead they take it
as a chance to pile grief on top of grief.

Enter MEDEA *from the house.*

MEDEA Our long wait for palace news is over.
One of Jason's servants sprints this way.
Listen, he gasps from exertion.
When he arrives expect to hear about disaster.

Enter servant of Jason's as MESSENGER.

MESSENGER Medea, such crimes, heinous—inhuman—   1090
You must go, now, by any means,
land or sea. Don't stay, fly!

MEDEA What's happened? Why should I escape?

72

MESSENGER   The princess and her father, Creon,
            lie dead, victims of your poison.

MEDEA   Splendid news! Let me reward you
        with my undying friendship and protection.

MESSENGER   Madness speaks through you.
            How can you slaughter Creon's family
            and then rejoice so fearlessly?   1100

MEDEA   There's an answer to your question—but first
        calm down, friend, and tell me
        about their deaths. Pay special attention
        to their agony so I might take some pleasure.

MESSENGER   The moment your sons with their father
            entered his bride's house, all of us,
            who once served you and who mourned
            your fate, were heartened. A shout went up
            that you and Jason had called a truce.
            This was like music to our ears. Suddenly,   1110
            we wanted to kiss the children, touch their
            lovely hair. Overwhelmed by happiness
            I followed them inside the princess's chambers.
            Understand, she's the woman we must serve
            instead of you.
                            At first she saw only Jason,
            but when the children came into view,
            she veiled her eyes, and turned away.
            Impatient with this display,
            your husband scolded her, saying:
            "Look at us. Don't revile your friends.   1120
            Your job is to love those your husband loves.
            They've brought gifts. Accept them graciously
            and for my sake ask your father to release
            these children from their exile."

            The gifts astonished her with their beauty.
            She agreed to what her husband asked.
            So eager was she to wear the treasures,

even before Jason and the boys had reached
the road, she put on the colorful dress,
set the gold crown on her head,   1130
and in a bright mirror arranged her hair.
She laughed with pleasure at the beautiful
but lifeless image. Then as if the gifts
had cast a spell, she stood up, dancing
through her rooms, giddy with the feel of the gown
twirling so she could see repeatedly
her shapely feet and pointed toes.

But soon her face changed color. She staggered,
legs trembling, almost collapsing
before she reached a chair. One of the older, wiser   1140
servants believed some wrathful god possessed her
and so cried out in prayer to Pan,
until she saw the mouth foaming,
eyes wild and rolling, and skin leached of blood.
Then the prayers turned shrill with horror
and we servants raced to find Creon
and Jason to tell them the piteous news,
filling the house with the sound
of our panicked feet.

All of this happened in less time   1150
than a sprinter takes to run the dash
and quicker still was the way the princess
from her terrible trance woke, eyes
wider than before, screaming
in anguish. For now a second torture
wracked her. The gold crown exploded
in a fiery ring about her head, while
the delicate gown, brought by your sons,
ate into her sweet flesh. Consumed by flames,
she stood and ran, shaking her head   1160
as if to throw the fire off, but the crown tangled
tighter in her hair and the blaze roared higher
as she fell to the floor and rolled
in the unquenchable flames.

Only her father could have known
who she was. The eyes had melted.
The face no more a face, while flaming blood
leaking from her head fueled the blaze.
But worse was how the flesh like tallow
or pitch sloughed off her bones.   1170
All of this because the viperous poison
had locked her in its invisible jaws.

Schooled by what we'd witnessed, none of us
would touch the body, but her father,
rushed to her side, not knowing what he'd find.
Nothing could prepare him for his daughter's
corpse. Misery broke from his voice.
He embraced and kissed her, lamenting,
"Unhappy child, murdered so shamefully,
why do the gods torture an old man like me?   1180
Daughter, let me die with you."
But when his sobbing ceased
and old Creon wanted to rise, he found
he was woven to the fatal dress, stitched
to it like ivy to laurel, unable
even as he wrestled furiously
to free himself. The living father,
who felt his flesh ripping from his bones,
could not match the strength of his dead daughter
and so he gave up and died, a victim   1190
of her hideous fortune. Together now they lie,
an old man and his daughter. Who wouldn't weep?

As for you, Medea, and your fate,
hear my silence. From it will come your punishment,
swift and sure. As for our brief lives, I've learned
once more we are mere shadows. No longer
do I fear to say the truth: Fine words
and clever plans breed folly.
No man can count on his happiness.
Some have luck and fortune on their side   1200
but never happiness.

Exit MESSENGER.

CHORUS   Today the gods delivered the justice
         Jason deserved and seized him with calamity.
         But the princess, a victim of marriage,
         now passing through the halls of death,
         we lament her terrible misfortune.

MEDEA   Nothing will undo my resolve
        to kill my children and escape
        —but it must be quick.
        If I hesitate now someone else   1210
        will murder them more cruelly.
        There's no way out. They must die.
        And I who gave them life will take it.
        Come, heart, shield yourself.
        Why doubt what must be done?
        Come, unlucky hand,
        grip the sword, carry it to where
        unhappiness begins and ends.
        Do not weaken.
        Forget you love your sons.   1220
        Forget you gave them life.
        Today, remember nothing.
        Tomorrow, mourn them.
        For even if you kill your sons,
        you once loved them dearly.
        My life has been all grief!

                                    Exit MEDEA *into the house.*

CHORUS   Earth, hear us! Bright sun, Helios,
            look down, expose Medea,
               before her sons are murdered
         by her bloody hands. Remember,   1230
            they are your radiant children. Remember,
         when men wound gods, fear and darkness rule
               over us.

Brilliant, heavenly light, burn up
    this murdering Fury. Banish her
from the house, cast out
    this servant of vengeance!

Wasted, the pain of bearing sons.
    Futile, their brief dear lives.
        Better not to have sailed the Black Sea,
escaped the Clashing Rocks. Why, Medea,   1240
    does rage cloud your mind?
        Why must murder follow murder?

When families kill their own, they spill
    no darker blood, leave no fouler stain.
And the gods drawn to its stench
    punish all who bear the family name.

CHILDREN   *Cries for help from within the house.*

CHORUS The children! Do you hear their awful pleas?
        Oh, wretched and afflicted woman!

FIRST CHILD Mother, no!
             Brother, help me!   1250

SECOND CHILD There's nothing I can do. We're trapped.

CHORUS If we went inside now we might stop the murder.

FIRST CHILD Yes, with the gods' help, save us!

SECOND CHILD Look, a knife!

CHORUS Only a stone or iron forged from ore
            is harder than your heart. If it weren't their fate
            could you bear to murder the children
            you brought into the world?

        Only Ino before you—of all women—
            killed her sons with her own hands.   1260

And she, deranged by Hera, was sent to wander
the ends of the earth in madness.
That's why she leapt into the sea.
That's why in her unholy plunge
she carried her murdered sons—and all perished.
What worse horror will we face
now that a woman's marriage bed
has bred again mortal pain and evil?

Enter JASON.

JASON You women, gathered near the door, tell me,
is Medea inside—such unspeakable crimes!
　　　　　　　　　　　　　　—or has she fled? 1270
She'll have to use the underworld to hide
or fly on wings to heaven to avoid what she deserves.
Murderess of the rulers of this land!
Does she think she'll leave this house alive?

But why should I care for her? It's the children
I'm looking for. She'll be punished.
Others will see to it, but I must protect my sons
from the revenge Creon's survivors are sworn
to make them suffer for their mother's crime.

CHORUS LEADER Jason, ignorant beyond pity, if you knew　　　1280
what lay ahead you'd never speak again.

JASON More treachery? Plans to murder me?

CHORUS LEADER With her own hands Medea killed your sons.

JASON What are you saying? This woman has destroyed
my life!

CHORUS LEADER I'm saying that your children are dead.

JASON Where did she do it? In the house? On the street?

CHORUS LEADER Behind these doors you'll find her slaughter.

JASON Call out the servants! Unlock the gates!
    First, I must see the murdered. Then I'll find Medea,
    the source of my disaster—   1290
    and seek revenge.

               JASON *tries to open the doors of the home.* MEDEA
               appears aloft in a chariot drawn by dragons.

MEDEA Why rattle the gates? Why open the house?
    You want the corpses? The murderer?
    Stop that banging! If it's me you're after, speak.
    Tell me what you want. Only words can reach me.
    Helios has sent his chariot to keep me from my
          enemies.

JASON Vilest woman! Condemned, hated by the gods,
    by me, and every human creature. No one
    but you raised the knife that butchered
    your children. No one but you destroyed   1300
    my life. How can you stand there
    and speak about the sacred Sun?
                 Guilty!
    Sentenced to die!
                       Now my mind is clear.
    How wrong I was to bring a barbarian home
    to Greece, already a dangerous betrayer
    of family and country. For this the gods have sent
    their Fury to torment me, though it was you
    who was cruel enough to kill your trusting brother,
    then leave with me aboard the noble Argo.
    That's how it started. Then we married.   1310
    Then you bore me children. The ones you've killed!
    All of this because of jealousy.
    Barbarians act like this, not Greeks.
    Yet I married a barbarian and yoked myself
    to hate and destruction.
    Compared to your brutal nature Scylla,
    with her heads and massive teeth,
    her many feet, is tame. Nothing hurts you.
    Insults and curses are praise.

Leave me, nothing worse than these murders   1320
can be done by you. My sorrowful fate
is my own: a bride's widower,
a childless father—all that I've worked
and planned for—lost.

MEDEA Why should I waste time replying to your words?
Zeus knows how I saved you and how
you repaid me with ingratitude.
Did you think that after you betrayed
our marriage you'd live a life of ease,
mocking me with Creon and his daughter,   1330
the princess he promised you before condemning me
to exile? Yes, call me fierce and vicious.
Say I'm a water fiend like Scylla—tell me,
how does it feel with my teeth in your heart!

JASON If you eat my heart, you swallow my pain.

MEDEA Pain without mockery is pleasure.

JASON My sons, you died at the hands of an evil mother.

MEDEA My sons, you died because of broken promises.

JASON My hand was not the one that raised the knife.

MEDEA No, the knife was whetted on your pride   1340
and the rails of your marriage bed.

JASON For pride and marriage you murdered sons?

MEDEA What woman would find your crime forgivable?

JASON A woman of sense, not a vengeful woman like you.

MEDEA Well, our sons are dead and that pain pierces your
          heart.

JASON No, they live on as Furies who will punish you.

80

MEDEA The gods understand the source of this violence.

JASON That means they fathom your gruesome heart.

MEDEA Go on, keep hating me, I detest your voice!

JASON And yours is worse. But I can end our argument.   1350

MEDEA How? Show me. I wish it too.

JASON Let me bury our sons. Let me mourn them properly.

MEDEA Impossible! My sons will be interred by me
       in the sacred ground of Hera Akraia, safe
       from my enemies who'd want to dig them up.
       And to expiate their murders, a solemn festival
       will be performed. Once these things are done,
       I'll go to Athens and live with Aegeus,
       my protector. But for you, justice is approaching.
       More miserable than now you'll die a coward,   1360
       your head crushed beneath a beam of the great Argo.
       Only then does the bitter story of our love end.

JASON May Fury and Justice, vengeful
       and murderous, tear you apart.

MEDEA Don't you know, gods are deaf to oath breakers
       and to those who deceive their guests.

JASON Defiled forever. Executioner!

MEDEA Go home to your wife. Go bury her.

JASON Yes, I'll go, grieving my sons.

MEDEA When you're old, grief that worsens day by day.   1370

JASON They were my beautiful boys!

MEDEA More beautiful to me, their mother.

JASON And so you murdered beauty?

MEDEA To give birth to your unending grief.

JASON If I could see them once more,
       I'd take them in my arms and kiss their mouths.

MEDEA Speak to them now?
       But you sent them away.

JASON Only to touch their soft skin, please . . .
       to hold my innocent children.   1380

MEDEA Impossible! Save your breath.

JASON Zeus, do you hear how I'm treated
       by this monster of filth and pollution
       who keeps me away from the children she murdered?
       All my life I will honor them with grief.
       I will call upon the mighty gods
       to remember how their killer denied
       my wish to lift them in my arms
       and place them in the earth. Now
       I regret their lives, for when I fathered them   1390
       I delivered them to a butcher's hands!

MEDEA *with the corpses of her children is borne aloft*
               away from Corinth. Exit JASON.

CHORUS LEADER The gods love surprise, so what men want
                   is often denied, and yet the gods prevail
               for us. Think of the story we've just listened to:
                   Who won? Who lost?
               Zeus stores our destinies in his great house,
                   some glitter brightly, but most are hidden.   1397

Exit Chorus.

NOTES ON THE TEXT

1–126 / 1–130 **Prologue.** Unusually, in this play the prologue proper — the Nurse's introductory speech, followed by spoken dialogue between the Nurse and her fellow slave, the Tutor — ends with a duet between Medea offstage and the Nurse onstage, which begins at line 86/96. Into this duet the Chorus of Corinthian matrons intrudes itself as a third voice at line 127/131 (see notes, lines 86–221/96–212 and 127–221/131–212).

1–39 / 1–48 Euripides' surviving plays usually begin with a long introductory speech by a leading character or god, designed to situate the audience in the action about to unfold. Only in *Medea* is this introductory speaker a solitary servant. The Nurse's age and affiliation with Medea's household and her knowledge of the past suggest that, in accordance with ancient practice, she may have been Medea's wet nurse and personal possession (see notes, lines 40/49 and 926–27/949 [=786]).

1 / 1 The opening of the play must have caught the ear and imagination of the Greeks, for twenty-five years later its first line appeared as Euripides' first entry in the verse weighing contest between himself and Aeschylus in Aristophanes' comedy *Frogs* (line 1382) and was ever afterwards cemented in the ancient poetic memory (cf., e.g., Catullus 64.171 ff.).

2 / 1 *wings* In ancient poetry flying metaphors were frequently used of beaked warships speeding like birds over the surface of the sea. Sometimes the billowing square-cut sails are envisioned as wings; at other times the rising and falling of the oars on either side of the hull as it cut through the water.

3 / 3–4 *the pines of Mt. Pelion* The Greek refers to a pine (*peukê*) — not pines — that turned heroes into oarsmen (literally "put oars in the hands of the best

men"). Since oars were not regularly made from pine — in Homer they are of silver fir (*Iliad* 7.5. *Odyssey* 12.172; cf. Theophrastus, *Enquiry into Plants* 5.1.7), in Virgil of oak (e.g., *Aeneid* 4.399–400) — but ships' hulls were (cf. Aristophanes, *Knights*, 1300–1310 and Theophrastus, *Enquiry into Plants* 5.7.1–2), it does not seem unreasonable to suppose that Euripides' seafaring audience would have imagined either that the hull of the Argo was made from one huge primeval pine or several pines, or that a single pine became her mast (cf. Lucan, *Pharsalia* 2.695). Legend had it that Athena herself had come to lofty Mount Pelion, above Iolcus, and with her own bronze ax had cut Argo's timbers. Indeed, the construction of this remarkable warship was a tale so well-known that Apollonius of Rhodes, the third-century BC author of the *Argonautica*, an epic in four books recounting the adventures of the Argonauts (Introduction, "Legendary Background"; notes, lines 481–82/480–82; Glossary, "Orpheus"), decided to skip it (*Argonautica* 1.18–19).

4 / 5 *heroes* Greek *aristoi andres*, or "best men." One of the extraordinary things about the Argo was that it was manned entirely by ancestral *aristoi*, who now, from the point of view of Euripides' audience, were each and every one a hero, a son or grandson of immortal gods. The heroic Argonauts contrasted sharply with fifth-century Athenian rowers, who were drawn from the lowest class of citizens, the "thêtes" or hired hands. As the "Old Oligarch" (a fifth-century BC political tract preserved among Xenophon's works and considered roughly contemporary with the composition of the *Medea*) confessed, it was their contribution to Athenian power that entitled this traditionally subject working class to the new political rights and power they now enjoyed under Athens' radical democracy. Is there, then, a trace of sarcasm in the Nurse's "heroes' oars"? See the Introduction, Historical Background.

8–9 / 9–10 *persuaded the daughters of Pelias to kill their father* Different literary sources give conflicting reasons as to why Jason was justified in killing Pelias; none explain why he and Medea must go into exile from Iolcus. The murder is a startling proof of Medea's frightening proficiency in sorcery. In order to convince the daughters of Pelias that she knows how to make their father young again, she puts the pieces of a dismembered old ram into a bubbling cauldron and then resurrects it whole and rejuvenated out of her potent stew. Eagerly Pelias's daughters try the same treatment on their beloved father, who, alas, fails to respond.

9–10 / 10 *living now in Corinth* The play tells us nothing about why Jason and Medea sought refuge with Creon in Corinth. Their exile status, which Euripides makes so much of, nevertheless contradicts earlier legends that connect both of them to the town. Jason's great Uncle Sisyphus was its legendary founder, but, according to Eumelus, a Corinthian poet of the eighth century BC, who wrote an epic history of the kings of Corinth, he succeeded to the throne only after Medea had held it in her own right. It seems Helios (the Sun) first gave Corinth to his son Aeëtes (Medea's father), who, before leaving for Colchis, entrusted its rule to Bounus (whoever he might be), until he himself or one of his descendants should return. When one of Bounus's heirs died childless, the Corinthians bestowed the town's rule upon Medea, and it was through her that Jason became king. Clearly Euripides ignores this genealogy to produce a new dramatic situation, perhaps more indicative of the political turmoil of his times. What happened to cause the death of their children is variously reported by different sources: out of hatred of her rule the Corinthians slaughter them, Medea kills them unintentionally, or she leaves them behind when she leaves Corinth and Creon's faction kills them, and so on. Common to all accounts is the fact that the children are remembered in an actual Corinthian cult. Thus, the cult of the children, also of importance to Euripides (lines 1353–57/1378–88), seems to be a fixed element in this otherwise fluid Corinthian myth.

15–16 / 19 *the daughter of Creon* Although unnamed in the play itself, the plot summary (*hypothesis*) affixed to the beginning of the *Medea* calls Creon's daughter Glauke (blue-eyed), a name apparently memorialized by the name of a sacred spring in Corinth into which she was said to have thrown herself to quench the malignant fire that was ravaging her body (see lines 1138 ff./1167 ff.). The name Creon simply means ruler and is used to designate place holders in a royal succession, such as Oedipus's successor in Sophocles' Theban plays.

40 / 49 The Nurse's interlocutor in the ensuing dialogue is another trusted servant whose primary duty, like that of the Nurse, concerned the care of Jason's and Medea's boys. This Tutor or, literally, "Escorter of Children" (*paedagogos*) accompanied his charges to and from school and had general oversight of them outside the house. Just as the main characters represent the noblest of the noble, so these household servants represent servile nobility. Their power in the house among their fellow slaves and their importance to and intimacy with their masters and their children are suggested by Plutarch (*Life of Alcibiades*, c. 1)

when he attests that the names of the Nurse and Tutor of the infamous
Alcibiades were known to posterity.

44 / 53 *Old tutor* Drawing attention to old age here and in the preceding greeting
may be intended not so much to enliven the servants' repartee as to
flesh out what is seen. In a huge outdoor theater in which the performers are lit by the sun, the details of a mask would be less visible
than the stance and gestures of the actor, and the visuals overall are
less individualizing than the clear auditory signals lodged in the
dialogue.

47–48 / 56–58 The sentiment is found repeatedly in ancient drama in the mouths
of characters who like the Nurse have to justify their uncustomary and
often improper public appearances (before the Chorus) outside the
palace.

61 / 70 *exile* Among the ancient Greeks, exile was considered almost as bad as de-
capitation, for an exile cut off from his family and city became almost
a nonperson. Like a beggar, he was reduced to living off the benevo-
lence of others.

68–69 / 78–79 Among these maritime peoples, the metaphor of the ship of state or,
in this case, of the great household is traditional, and, not surprisingly,
it is prominent in this play about the shipwreck of the Argo's
commander.

86–221 / 96–212 At this point the Greek meter changes from iambic (spoken) to
anapestic (sung and declaimed or chanted) verse, as Medea offstage
sings of her woe and Jason's treachery, and the Nurse in response comments upon what she hears, using a more elevated vocalization to
match the musicality and more insistent tempo of the anapestic meter.
Later, when the Chorus adds its voice to their exchange, what seemed
to be a duet is transformed into a regular antiphonal *kommos*, a lyrical
interchange between the actors and chorus. It is probable, based on
Medea's use of rounded ah's (Doric dialect) instead of the Nurse's flat
ay's (Athenian or Attic dialect, regularly used in the spoken iambics of
Attic tragedy) that Medea sings and the Nurse declaims. The anapestic
meter sets up a marching rhythm and so is a natural accompaniment
to the Chorus's entrance song or *parodos* (see notes, lines 127–221/131–
212).

This passage and the other lyric passages of this play were accompanied by a single piper playing on *auloi*, that is, twin reed pipes (like oboes or clarinets), which were played as a pair, each of the *aulete's* hands fingering one of the two pipes.

127–221 / 131–212 Parodos. Fifteen high-born Corinthian matrons now add their voices to those of the Nurse and Medea, first with sung anapests as they march into the orchestra (the theater's large circular dancing floor at the foot of the South slope of the Acropolis upon which the audience is sitting), and then with two matching stanzas (see notes, lines 148–58/148–59) in the mixed lyric meters characteristic of choral odes. After the Nurse leaves the stage to fetch Medea, they sing a third stanza to mark the end of the play's preparatory action and the beginning of the first episode.

Choruses sang a single melodic line—polyphony and harmony in our sense of these words were as yet unknown—in a one-to-one ratio between notes and syllables of text, and their range did not exceed an octave. Thus, their lyrics would have been more readily understood by the audience than those of modern choruses. Whether the male choristers sang in a falsetto when impersonating females, we have no idea. Choral song was accompanied by mimetic dancing, whose movements are unrecoverable.

127 / 131, *I heard her voice* Despite the use of the first person singular, the Chorus is singing collectively as it enters from the wings. "I" and "we" seem to be used interchangeably in choral lyrics.

131–33 / 138 Lyrical lamentations, sung by a distraught main character are an essential, almost ritualized feature of Attic tragedy. When the tragic chorus participates in them and they occur at the beginning of the action, the collective chorus often acts conventionally as comforters to the soloist. To make their exchange dramatically convincing, the playwright often highlights some plausible prior ground of allegiance between them. Here, because Medea is a foreigner and the Chorus are natives and, consequently, their friendship cannot be taken for granted, they explain their friendly visit by referring to the goodwill they owe her in return for previous benefactions to them. Friendship, especially between strangers, is not so much a matter of affection as of a network of obligations. Medea was useful to Jason because she could perform favors for the Corinthians that made them obliged to him. Presumably the women represent their husbands' or fathers' houses in a kind of parallel "female polis"; they need not like Medea.

144 / 144 *Zeus's thunderbolts kill* An expansion of the Greek *phlox ourania* (heavenly flame or lightning), the invincible weapon by which Zeus, the king of the gods, rules the universe. The chorus picks up this theme in its response, "O Zeus, and Earth and Light . . ." (line 148/148)

148–58 / 148–59 Choral odes in Attic tragedy commonly consist of one or more paired strophes and antistrophes. Each strophe (or "turn," a dance term in origin?) is answered by an antistrophe (counterturn), which is rhythmically—and presumably melodically—the same. Thus, the chorus dances and sings a turn, then a matching counterturn, usually following immediately upon the turn but in this case postponed until after the Nurse's and Medea's anapests.

148 / 148 Zeus guarantees justice (see notes, lines **155–56/157** and **344 ff./324 ff.**), Earth sends forth her avengers against the forsworn, and the Light of Day (or the Sun) sees all wrongdoing. This divine triad is often called upon to witness oath taking.

155–56 / 157 *Trust in Zeus* Zeus is preeminently the god of Justice (*Dikê*, see the Glossary, "Themis" and "Zeus") who keeps watch over the right ordering of the universe, secures equitable distributions and alliances among gods and men, and punishes wrongdoers. The Greek implies that Zeus will be Medea's advocate in her just cause against Jason.

160–62 / 166–67 The Greek says simply "I departed in shame, having killed my brother." However, the story of Medea's strewing the fleeing Argo's wake with bits of her slaughtered brother Apsyrtus in order to delay her father, who piously stopped to collect each precious limb, presents such a compelling image that commentators often assume that Medea alludes to it here. This gruesome version is generally attributed to Pherecydes, a mid-fifth-century BC Athenian genealogist, but may actually have originated with Sophocles in a lost play *Scythians*, which recounts the return voyage of the Argo (see H. Lloyd-Jones comments in his 1996 Loeb Sophocles III, pp. 274–77). We do not know, however, whether this undatable version was already circulating when Euripides wrote the *Medea*; he, in any case, seems to have another version in mind (see lines **1307–9/1334–35**, with note).

163–70 / 160–65 Medea takes up the theme, suggested by the Chorus, of the mighty oath that Jason once swore and now has broken. She invokes Themis, an archaic personification whose name, "Law" or "Custom" (literally, "That which has been established"), implies that she is a guardian of the prohibitions and prescriptions that regulate the affairs of men (and . gods), especially those of divine or primordial origin.

Artemis, the virgin huntress leading her train of dancing nymphs through the wilds, is often depicted in myth as the slayer of young women, a reminder of the risks girls face when they become brides and new mothers. Perhaps she is called upon here to be Medea's savior, both in memory of what she once was when she first bound Jason to herself and entered upon motherhood and as the destroyer of his new wife. It may be that Artemis is also invoked here because of her association with the goddess Hecate (see note, line 415/395–97)

198–212 / 190–203 To Greeks, music as a way of forgetting cares was proverbial.

220–21 / 210–13 *through the impassable maw that guards the way to Greece* The Bosporus.

222–447 / 214–409 First Episode.

222–84 / 214–266 In sharp contrast to her previous wailing, when Medea now comes through the palace doors of the temporary scene building, her polite and politic words give to modern readers the impression of calm self-control. This sudden change from fire to ice has been rationalized in many ways, sometimes in terms of Medea's character, psyche, or personality (she is the kind of woman who under these circumstances is able with great effort to rein in her emotions), sometimes according to formal variations between impassioned lyrics and supposedly rational deliberations. Still others have called attention to the sophistical quality of her rhetoric with its indirect generalities.

285–89 / 267–70 The Chorus is now speaking (in iambics), not singing. Whenever this occurs, it is thought that only the Chorus Leader speaks.

288–89 / 269–70 Creon appears with a small retinue (cf. line 355/335). Both Aegeus and Jason may also have retinues.

344–60 / 324–39 Formal line by line interchanges between two characters are typical of Greek tragedy, particularly in contexts of debate and cross-examination.

344 ff. / 324 ff. *I beg you* At this point, or, as some critics maintain, at line 356/336, Medea kneels in a formal act of supplication and grasps Creon's knees (in the Greek) and right hand. By following these rituals, she puts herself and her claim to Creon's favor under the protection of Zeus as god of suppliants (*Hikesios/Hiketesios*). This is another way in which Zeus secures justice for the weak in the face of brute force.

377 / 356 This play, contrary to contemporary fashion and Euripides' usual practice, does not require the usual three actors, but like earlier tragedies could be performed throughout by just two actors. If indeed it was so performed, the actor playing Creon would exit at this point to change into the Jason mask and costume. (Only in the prologue, when Medea sings from within, is a third voice required, and that voice need not have belonged to a third actor. Any good singer would do—the poet himself, for example—and, since Medea does not sing on stage, the audience need not have noticed the difference between the unseen singer's third voice and the voice of the actor on stage intoning Medea's spoken lines.)

401–2 / 383 *They'd mock and laugh at me intolerably* It is not death per se she fears, but their gloating laughter and her degradation. See also lines 772/781–82, 787–88/797, 1026–27/1049–50, and 1330/1355, and Introduction, "Medea's honor."

407–9 / 386–90 These lines prepare us for the arrival of Aegeus later in the play.

415 / 395–97 *Hecate* Euripides' *Medea* is our earliest evidence for Hecate in her classic role as the sinister goddess of magic and sorcery, by whose secret nocturnal rites a privileged few, her priests and priestesses, gained access to the Underworld with its disembodied souls and hidden lore. Like other purveyors of novel mysteries who were then flocking to Periclean Athens, Medea keeps a shrine to her special goddess in the innermost reaches of her home, presumably as a repository for the rare and potent drugs (*pharmaka*) that, with the goddess's help, she has harvested at times and places suitable for contact with dangerously polluting demonic powers (see Introduction, "Medea's character").

The exclusivity of Medea's mysteries contrasts with popular cult, in which both public and private shrines were placed at the entrances to cities and houses, along roadways near graves, and especially at crossroads, those dangerous points of contact between lower- and upper-world forces where triformed Hecate of the Crossroads (*Enodia, Triod-itis*) was thought to dwell. Here, when the moon was full, her devotees would make offerings of shiny cakes. Conversely, at midnight on starlit new moon nights they would set out strange prophylactic sacrifices, called "Hecate's dinners," whose contents seem to have included kneaded cakes and puppies or fish.

Hecate appears in two forms in Greek art, as single-faced and Artemis-like with torches and hounds and, when her nature as Mistress of the Crossroads is being emphasized, in triplicate, sometimes with three heads on one body but more often with three full images facing outward from a central pole, a type immortalized in a famous statue of Alcamenes, set up in Athens about the time of the *Medea's* first performance.

432–47 / 410–45 First Stasimon. This is the first of five choral odes sung and danced by the Chorus in front of the scene building. They are called stasima or "standing" odes, presumably because the Chorus begins and ends its movements in a standing position, possibly a squared military formation three files deep.

432 / 410 The Chorus mentions a reversal of nature that ancient magicians (like Medea) claimed to be able to effect (cf. Virgil, *Aeneid* 4.489; Ovid. *Metamorphoses*, 7.199–200).

436–37 / 421–23 *ancient songs that sing our faithlessness* Commentators usually cite lines from Hesiod or the invective of Semonides as illustrations of the contumely heaped upon women, but I think the reference here is most probably to epic tales. The queen of faithlessness is Helen, but there are others, like Phaedra or Clytemnestra, and Aphrodite herself, the teacher of untrustworthy seduction. Not to be forgotten among treacherous women is, ironically, Medea.

438–39 / 424–26 *Apollo* As Lord of the Lyre, the shining god (Phoebus) Apollo leads the Chorus of the Muses, daughters of Memory (the oral tradition) and goddesses of song and choral dance. *Mousikê*, his province, embraces more than the knowledge of the tunings of the lyre, melodies, or rhythms; it embraces the winged words themselves, messengers of the divine knowledge of the past, present, and future that epic bards dispensed. That Apollo does not let this Chorus "carry a tune" (Collier, line 438, in Greek "did not grant the inspired song of the lyre," lines 424–425) indicates that they have not gone to school.

448–633 / 446–626 Second Episode. The real world analog of the explosive *agon* ("contest" of paired antagonistic set speeches) with which this episode begins is to be found in the formalities and vitriolic, highly personal atmosphere of the Athenian law courts—a speech of prosecution (Medea) spoken by or on behalf of the victim, answered by the accused's own defense (Jason)—with two notable concessions to the dramatic milieu: overwrought women did not appear in courts on their own behalf and the introductory remarks designed to elicit the jury's sympathy and goodwill are lacking.

448–66 / 446–64 The tone of these lines is hard to fix. One can imagine them as conveying officiousness, "nauseating self-righteousness" (Elliott), or "ineffable smugness" (Morwood). One can even imagine a sympathetic rendering in which a sorrowful and frustrated husband tries to deal with an hysterical and intractable woman. Contemporary audiences, persuaded by the affecting directness of Medea's first speech whose justice they feel, find her a sympathetic character and Jason incomprehensible, if not downright reprehensible. But ancient Greeks would not have been so repelled. The citizenship law of 451 BC, which decreed that Athenians had to prove that both their parents were citizens, made the disadvantages of a foreign marriage for one's children keenly felt. As heads of households, men legally ruled their wives and believed that a woman's greatest assets were temperance and submissiveness, virtues Medea clearly lacks. It was considered dangerous for a man to contract an alliance with a wealthier, higher class, smarter woman, since she was more likely to rule him than to be ruled. Thus, though Jason was clearly in the wrong for having broken his oath, the men in the audience would not have been as unreceptive as moderns to his excuses.

477–78 / 476 The Greek of line 476—"*esôsa s' hôs isasin Hellênôn hosoi.*" (I saved you, as all the Greeks know who . . .)—was famous for its (snaky, hissing) sibilants, which were designed to grate on the ear. Medea is spitting mad.

481–82 / 480–82 *I killed the . . . serpent* In Pindar's Fourth Pythian Ode, an earlier account of the legend of the Argo, Jason, not Medea, kills the dragon (line 249). Apollonius of Rhodes, writing a century and a half later, has Medea put the dragon to sleep. Such variants are typical of the fluidity of ancient myth.

481 ff. / 480 ff. Medea omits her brother's murder (see line 160/167) from this catalogue of the benefits she has conferred upon Jason. A good lawyer never

brings forward facts that can have negative implications for his client, and Medea, as the audience already knows, speaks like a well-trained and effective advocate.

497–99 / 496–98 Breaking his oath is Jason's greatest offense against the gods. In the Greek, without mentioning supplication per se, Medea refers to her right hand and knees, thus immediately reminding her audience (and Jason) that Jason had knelt to her in formal supplication, just as she has just knelt to Creon. Because this custom with its symbolic gesture of submission, whereby the kneeling petitioner clasps the right hand (of honor and power) and knees of the one being petitioned, is foreign to modern English speakers, Collier substitutes another familiar act of submission, bowing the head, for "knees," and overtly names Jason as a "supplicant."

Interestingly, Apollonius makes Medea, not Jason, the suppliant; she begs that he take her away with him.

527–28 / 520–21 In formalized debates, choruses often offer neutral comment to mark the transition from one speech to the next.

533–39 / 526–31 The idea, first exampled here, that love, not the perpetrator, is the true cause of an action was a rhetorical commonplace favored by sophists in practice or display speeches, most notably in defenses of Helen of Troy. Euripides has Helen herself use it in the *Trojan Women* (lines 940 ff.) of 415 BC, and it is also found in a famous "Encomium (Praise) of Helen" by the brilliant and influential sophist Gorgias of Leontini (in Sicily) who, we are told, came as an ambassador to Athens in 427 BC, soon after the production of the *Medea*.

545–46 / 537–38 *Justice, not force, rules here* Barbarians who are the slaves of the Great King must serve his pleasure (cf. Herodotus 7.79 where the Colchians are part of the invading Persian army), but free Greeks obey only their city's laws. On the other hand, at the time of this play, recent decrees promulgated by a sovereign Athenian assembly were seen by many to be blatantly unjust, an irony that may extend to Jason's own claims and actions with regard to Medea. He broke his oath, and she can find no Greek law to protect her.

550 / 543 Orpheus is mentioned by Jason here not only as a fellow Argonaut, but because he, like Medea, was the proud possessor of powerful occult wisdom—knowledge of Underworld mysteries, incantation, and, indeed, the entire nature of things both human and divine. This wisdom, the know-how to make things happen, not just to entertain with delightful sounds, made Orpheus's voice worth coveting. By the fifth century BC there was in Greece a body of oracular hexameter poetry—cosmogonies, revelations, healing spells, purifications, and so on—circulating under his name, promulgated by secret "Pythagorean" societies that practiced various forms of abstinence and held out the promise of a blessed life after death to those who had been initiated into the highest level of divine science.

569–70 / 563–64 *sons . . . brothers to ours, not rivals* Jason is assuring Medea that her sons will not be disinherited. Under the new Athenian marriage law (see notes, lines 448–66/446–64, and Introduction, "Medea's honor") their legitimacy might have been questioned; but clearly under ancestral law they would have kept their rights as *his* sons and heirs to *his* lands (in Iolcus and elsewhere), though, to be sure, they would not be eligible to inherit Creon's estate and power, as would Jason's sons by the princess.

572–73 / 565 *Children are more important to fathers than to mothers* (in Greek, "Why do you need [more] children?") Since mothers were technically outsiders (*thuraioi*) to their husbands' and children's houses and could themselves own no property or be heads of households, a woman could not enlarge her own wealth or her husband's family's prosperity by marrying a second spouse and adding his sons to sons she might already have. Once a woman had borne two sons—one to care for her in her old age and to guarantee her status as a mother in his household, and one to serve as a spare, in case the first son died—then she had as many as she needed. More than two would diminish the wealth of the house in which she would eventually reside once her husband was dead. For Jason and most ancient Greeks the importance of children derived not from parental affection but from the fact that, even more than fame and glory, they (especially the males) were tangible sureties of their father's own immortality and of the enduring power and prestige of his house. Though Medea once was the cause of the success of Jason's house, she is now irrelevant to its prosperity (or so Jason supposes), since he has found a more materially rewarding alliance elsewhere.

575–83 / 568–75 That women are slaves to the pleasures of sex is a commonplace of classical literature. The protagonist of Euripides' *Hippolytus* makes a similar protest against the need for women in order to beget children (*Hipp.* 616 ff.).

584–86 / 576–78 The Chorus, like the disinterested Aegeus later on, finds Jason's deeds blameworthy, representing perhaps a naive but normative rejection of Jason's rhetoric.

600 / 591 *barbarian* The Greek "barbaros" means anyone who was not a Greek by language or race. Since the Persian wars, barbarian slaves, whose presence in Athens was quite noticeable—for instance, the police were Scythians—had been deemed slavish, not just in their submission to their masters but also in their lack of self-control. Without the benefit of a true Hellenic education, they could be neither good nor beautiful. Their dress, their strange manners, even their attempts to speak Greek were mocked on the comic stage.

618–19 / 612–13 These lines remind the audience of the power and high status of Jason's house throughout the Greek world and beyond. A literal translation of the Greek—". . . I am ready . . . to send tokens (*symbola*) to my guest-friends elsewhere in Greece, who will treat you well"—reveals a reference to a specific Greek custom: upon the completion of an agreement or contract, either unique (or rare) objects were exchanged or, more commonly, an object was broken into two (or more) dovetailing pieces and each party was given one of these unique pieces, as proof of the holder's legitimate interest in the deal. In this instance, the agreement was one of "guest-friendship" (*xenia*), a pact of mutual assistance or an alliance between two noble houses of different cities. Through such an agreement, influential exiles, though parted from their friends and denied their accumulated honors and political rights at home, could rely upon family guest-friendships to provide refuge and a base of operations.

634–57 / 627–62 **Second Stasimon.** The Chorus picks up the thematic thread of excessive passion from Medea's closing statement and gives it general application. By doing so, it evokes her earlier intemperate love for Jason. The first system of strophe and antistrophe (see notes, lines 148–58/148–59) uses one complex metrical pattern, the second system another. The second strophe and antistrophe turn from intemperate Love as the cause of Medea's betrayal of her father and city to her present situation, as one bereft of city and friends. As usual, the Chorus provides supplemental generalizing comment on the action, rather than contributing to it. With the appearance of Aegeus and his grant of asylum, we soon discover, however, that this picture of an abject Medea is false. A person with her extraordinary powers can always buy another friendship.

658–815 / 663–823 Third Episode.

This scene is famously condemned by Aristotle: "It is right, however, to censure both improbability and depravity where there is no necessity and no use is made of the improbability. An example is Euripides' introduction of Aegeus or (of depravity) the character of Menelaus in the *Orestes*" (*Poetics* xxv 1461b 19–21, tr. W. Hamilton Fyfe [Loeb]). If Aristotle is actually referring to our play and not some other lost play— we know of one called *Aegeus*—he seems to have in mind the accidental, unmotivated way in which (a less than heroic) Aegeus and Medea meet halfway through the action. The Athenian king just happens to be passing through Corinth on his way from Delphi to Troezen; she just happens to be standing there for no particular reason, a happenstance with no justification in the received tradition (*Poetics* 1461b 14–15 and cf. 60b 35–61a 3). Indeed, the received tradition seems to be altogether against it, since Theseus, not Aegeus, was considered an Argonaut and Jason's contemporary. Furthermore, the meeting might be thought to serve no vital purpose: a heroine with Medea's talents and supernatural connections hardly needs a rescuer, and her intractable anger guarantees that she will punish Jason and Creon regardless of the aftermath.

In Euripides' defense, moderns have offered compensating dramatic reasons for bringing the clueless Aegeus so unexpectedly onto the stage: His dialogue with Medea provides a sharp contrast to the preceding agon. Unlike Jason, he respects her, recognizes her wisdom, confirms her judgment of Jason's wickedness, and swears an honorable oath to provide her with sanctuary. She, on the other hand, is shown, less sympathetically than before, to be a woman as willing to manipulate this honest, unsuspecting man for her own ulterior devices as she is her enemies. All of these dramatic justifications are quite reasonable, especially if one takes into account the dramatic force of surprise. More provocative and anti-Aristotelian is the argument that the Aegeus scene is actually essential to the plot, on the grounds that, since Medea announces that she will kill her children only after the Aegeus scene, her decision must have been prompted by Aegeus's desire to remedy his childlessness. Before this scene she is still uncertain of her methods, and even asserts that she will kill Jason (lines 393–94/375); after it her plans are set. She will kill her own children, not Jason, since killing them will accomplish more than killing him: it will destroy his whole house. This logical connection between Aegeus's childlessness and Jason's is, however, completely absent from Medea's dialogue, which is the only sure evidence of her reasoning process. All that Medea says — and the Chorus offers no contrary evidence — is that Aegeus has provided her, not the children (cf. line 793), with a "safe harbor." She will kill them not just to destroy Jason's house, but because she will not leave them behind in the hands of her enemies.

Aristotelian probabilities and plot construction aside, there is another obvious reason for Aegeus's appearance: the Athens connection. Aegeus was a founding king of Athens and the father of Athens' greatest hero, Theseus. The bargain that Medea strikes with him, to the detriment of the Corinthians, has aetiological value. It explains why Corinth becomes Athens' enemy. Perhaps the generous, righteous, yet ultimately gullible Aegeus is a convenient precursor of the timely, patriotic, and cautionary "Athens Ode" (Third Stasimon, 816–49/824–65). In other words, the patriotic value of the Aegeus scene provided Euripides with sufficient motivation and his audience with sufficient delight to overcome its inherent improbabilities.

662 / 667 *Delphi—Apollo's oracle* Apollo alone understood the mind of Zeus and, when inquiries were made at his temple at Delphi, a sanctuary centrally located in a steep mountain pass above the north shore of the Gulf of Corinth, he transmitted bits of this complete knowledge to the Pythia, a ritually pure prophetess who in an ecstatic trance intoned messages from the beyond.

674 / 679 *Choke off the wineskin's spout* The plain meaning of the oracle, that Aegeus is not to get drunk or have sex before reaching home, seems not to accord with the legend of Theseus's birth as we know it. See next note.

677 / 682 Not necessarily on his way home to Athens from Delphi, but certainly on his way to Troezen, Aegeus would have passed through Corinth. If we can trust Medea's wishes for his success (683/688; 747/756) and the absence of any obvious clues to the contrary, undeterred by his profitable encounter with Medea, he will continue his journey to Troezon, where Pittheus, wise to the intent of the oracle, will see to it that Aegeus becomes drunk (unchokes the wineskin's spout) and, as a result, sleeps with (unchokes the wineskin's spout) Pittheus's daughter Aethra *before* he returns to Athens. Theseus, the greatest of Athens' heroic forebears, is the offspring of this union.

How is it possible, moderns ask, for Aegeus to beget an heir in Troezen when the oracle expressly forbids his having intercourse before reaching Athens? Since Euripides seems not to have invented the oracle—a presumably earlier epic version is preserved in Plutarch's *Life of Theseus*—it is likely that the Greeks did not read it as a prohibition, but as indicating that the next time Aegeus had intercourse he would beget an heir. Pittheus's wisdom lay not just in understanding this but in ensuring that Medea would not be the mother of the prophesied heir. The story of Medea in Athens and her attempt to murder Theseus was the subject of two undatable plays called *Aegeus*, one by Sophocles, the other by Euripides himself. Aethra, Theseus's mother, is a main character in Euripides' *Suppliants*.

684 / 689 *tears* By her verbal delivery or by some gesture or altered posture, Medea elicited this response. Tears would not have been visible through a mask or even on a naked face, considering the distance between the ancient audience and the actor. They were made evident by Aegeus's words.

717–24 / 725–30 If Medea comes freely as a suppliant to Aegeus, he can honor Zeus Hikesios (protector of suppliants), like the righteous man he is, and protect her, without violating his guest-friendships with Creon and Jason and the house of Pelias. But if he were to help her flee Corinth, he would be transgressing these older alliances that, like all foreign alliances, were protected by the enforcing might of Zeus Xenios (protector of hospitality). As one who had broken faith with his Corinthian hosts, he would have merited their revenge.

725–26 / 731–32 Medea says, in effect, that it's time to bring on the lawyers. The language of oath is the ancient Greek equivalent of our written contract law, a protection for all parties concerned. Since for the Greeks the enforcement of law was ultimately the responsibility of the gods, an oath, calling upon the gods as sureties, added real binding force to the proceedings. The ensuing oath taking suggests the original oath taking between Jason and Medea. As in that earlier contract, she now promises Aegeus the effective use of her drugs if he will accept her into his house as her protector (*kyrios*). Aegeus's promise to Medea (deliberately, out of politeness?) obscures what legend supplied, namely, that she would become his concubine—not marry her surely, as he already has a wife (line 668/673). See Introduction, "Medea's honor."

729 / 734 *Pelias's sons* In Greek "the house of Pelias," which would include Pelias's sons-in-law (see note on lines 8–9/9–10 and Introduction, "Legendary background") and grandsons, as well as his celebrated son Acastus.

737–38 / 746–47 In his daily passage across the sky, Helios, the sun, the all-seeing eye of Zeus, espies evildoers and reports their activities to his master. The whole race of gods is a conventional fail-safe in oath taking, in case whoever swears later alleges that his oath was not binding because some other god, by whom he should have been sworn, was overlooked. Such procedural mistakes could be used to invalidate an agreement, sometimes long after the fact.

740–46 / 749–55 Oaths must be specific; the vaguer they are, the more easily they are abrogated. Curses were routinely added to oaths to strengthen them.

746 / 755 *others who renounce them* Those who failed to respect the gods properly, the *dus-seboi*, were liable to prosecution for impiety under Attic law (this is what happened to Socrates), and, if convicted, they suffered severe punishments (divine and human) that had serious consequences, often beyond a single generation. Pericles' mother's family, the Alcmaeonidae (called the Accursed), were under a curse two centuries old, because an ancestor had wrongfully killed certain suppliants. (See Herodotus 5.71 and Thucydides 1.126.)

772 / 782 *targets for my enemies* The Greek for targets, *kathybrisai*, refers to the ways her enemies in Corinth will insult and degrade, even harm, her defenseless children, who are their enemies, by virtue of their kinship with her. On the ancient honor code and the power of *hybris*, see Introduction, "Medea's honor" (cf. the passages listed with the note on 401–2/383).

775 / 786 *one priceless gown* The Doric *peplos* was a simple overgarment, a rectangular piece of woolen cloth draped like a tunic and secured at the shoulders. The adjective *leptos*, here "priceless," indicates the fineness of the thread and the overall delicacy of the cloth.

784 / 794 *bring down Jason's house* This formula was common to curses. Medea will be the instrument of the curse that would have been placed on Jason at the time of their oath taking. Annihilation of a man's house entailed erasing its wealth, honor, and male progeny. Thus, to kill an

enemy's male children was the right of an avenger. What is unusual here is that the enemy's children are the avenger's own.

787–88 / 797 *easier to bear than my enemies who mock me* We may find it incredible that Medea would kill her children to forestall her enemies' laughter at her expense, but our sensibilities are not attuned, as the Greeks' were, to the demands of a militant shame-culture in which Achilles destroys many sturdy Greek souls just to make Agamemnon pay for his bullying and Ajax kills himself because he cannot endure the disgrace of his comrades' gloating. (Cf. the passages listed in the note on 401–2/383.)

803–5 / 811–13 Medea finally loses the Chorus's goodwill when she announces her decision to kill her own children (line 783/792–93).

812–15 / 820–23 The Nurse, who is addressed here, must have been a silent figure by Medea's side during the preceding action, perhaps having come out of the house with her before her first speech. It is possible that, while the Nurse goes off in another direction to look for Jason, Medea exits through the center door. Possible, but unlikely, since the second system of the next choral ode is addressed to her. Still, an exit at this point would give Medea the opportunity to ready her poisonous gifts, and she could reenter in time for the Chorus to address her in their lyrics. But if she misses the first system, how can she make sense of the second, which begins with a conclusion based on the first?

816–49 / 824–65 **Third Stasimon**, referred to as the "Athens Ode" (see note on the Third Episode, lines 658–815/663–823, and the Introduction, "Historical background"). Serious ideas about Athens and the nature of things lie behind the conceits of the first two stanzas (first strophe and antistrophe).

816–18 / 824–26 *Children of the gods, of sacred Earth, since ancient times, Athenians have flourished, unconquered* Erechtheus, from whom all Athenians claimed descent, was born from the Earth, begotten by Hephaestus (god of fire, metalworking, and other crafts), and raised by Athens' patron goddess Athena (bestower of prowess in war, wisdom, and weaving). He married the granddaughter of the River Cephisus, who like all rivers is a deity. The Athenians were proud of the fact that they were born from the earth (*autochthonoi*); that is, not immigrants. The notion was emphasized by sponsors of the democracy, because it made even lower-class citizens somehow landed nobility and worthy of rule.

818–20 / 826–30 *nourished by the vivid air that brings them grace and wisdom* The image is more concrete than we might realize, for progressive thinkers of the day believed that human intelligence comes from a tangible divine nature manifest in the air and light around us. Even in later Greek thought, *pneuma* (breath, wind, spirit) at its finest is not to be differentiated from light or intelligible fire (*aether*). The theme of purified and intelligent air is taken up in a different way in the antistrophe (see next note).

823–29 / 835–45 Since the River Cephisus, unlike the Illissus, did not dry up in summer, even at the hottest time of year it could be the source of air-tempering moisture. A climate most favorable to the good health and moral perfection of living beings was thought to depend upon the proper mixture of purifying sunlight, air, and moisture. Thus, here Aphrodite, fashioner of living things and goddess of all mixing, wreathed in roses (her signature flowers), blends air and Cephissan water, the dry and the moist, to concoct a perpetual life-giving, soul-enhancing, creativity-sustaining springtime. She does this in her cosmic breathing, which mimics human respiration.

850–952 / 866–975 Fourth Episode.

926–27 / 949 [=786] A woman's clothing and jewelry—possibly also her personal slaves—were hers to dispose of as she wished, unlike the rest of her dowry, which was controlled by her husband (Sealey, *Women and Law in Classical Athens*, pp. 26–27).

931–32 / 954–55, *heirlooms that Helios . . . bequeathed* Yet another allusion to Medea's kinship with Helios, a sign of her portentous access to potent Underworld magic. Gold, a solidified liquid (cf. Plato, *Timaeus* 59B), retains the fiery qualities of its original molten state and is emblematic of Helios's original nature.

953–76 / 976–1001 Fourth Stasimon. This song notably lacks the general utterances that predominate in the first strophic pairs of the first three Choruses. Close linkage to the action at hand complements the heightened pace and helps alter the tonal register of the proceedings as Medea implements her vengeance.

977–1056 / 1002–80 **Fifth Episode.**

1003–05 / 1026–27 A child's marriage was the final maternal duty, and ancient mothers exulted in the part they played in the wedding ceremonies. As heads of housekeeping, they would have had oversight of the ritual bath taken by the bride and groom before dressing for their nuptials, and, in the case of the mothers of the bride, of the smooth running of the banquet at the bride's father's house, where the formal unveiling of the bride before the groom took place. The climax of the nuptials came when the groom took his bride from her father's house and here, after the young couple, the bride's mother held pride of place. Raising torches aloft, she led the procession of well-wishers who, with song and dance and shouts of congratulations, escorted the newlyweds to the groom's house. There, at the door, she ceded her honors to the groom's mother, who with torches newly lit from her son's hearth, greeted him and welcomed her daughter-in-law to her new home. A mother's lamentations, like Medea's here, that she will not participate in this blessed event because of her or her children's death are common to tragedy.

1006 / 1028 *My unforgiving self has made me wretched* Medea here finally confesses the fault of which she has been accused by all others in the play (save Aegeus), her *authadeia*, her unshakeable determination to carry out her will and satisfy her implacable anger. See Introduction, "Medea's character."

1026–27 / 1049–50 Medea's dread of being laughed at by her enemies again; cf. the passages listed in the note for lines 401–2/383.

1029–31 / 1053–55 Medea is sending her children into the house as sacrificial animals. The language reflects the often-heard formula warning the profane or impure to keep away from sacred rites, whose performance their presence would invalidate or corrupt.

1032–56 / 1056–80 Some critics have regarded these lines as an interpolated doublet of lines 1040–55, ill-adjusted to the context. Others have disputed this radical surgery and bracketed some lines, but not others. This translation assumes the lines are genuine and makes them dramatically plausible.

1035–36 / 1059 *Hell's vengeful demons* In Greek "the netherworld avengers (*alastores*) in Hades," that is, the Furies.

1054–56 / 1078–80 *Angry passions have mastered me — emotions of misrule that destroy
men* The Greek reads "I understand the kind of evil I shall bring myself
to perpetrate, but my anger (*thumos*), which is the cause of the greatest
evils for mortals, is stronger than my counsels (*bouleumata*)." Stoics
used these lines to illustrate their belief that the rational soul acts as a
unit in coming to all decisions. By their account, Medea, fully con-
scious of which path she is about to take and even that it is the wrong
one, nevertheless deliberately chooses vengeance on Jason over saving
the children. In rebuttal, Platonists, who believed the passionate part
of the soul to be in conflict with the rational part, took the lines to
mean that Medea's anger is stronger than her right reasoning (John
M. Dillon in Clauss/Iles Johnson, 1997, pp. 211–18). Either way, the
ancient debate proves that these lines were established in the Greek
text by the third century BC and shows that the word "counsels" was
taken to refer not to her plotting throughout the play (as some scholars
think), but to her present advice to herself that she ought not kill her
children.

1057–85 / 1081–1115 If Medea exited with the children at 1056/1080, then the Chorus
Leader speaks to an empty stage. These comments in declaimed ana-
pests, similar to those uttered by the Nurse (lines **86–221/96–212** ff.),
mark an interlude during which neither Chorus nor audience knows
what is happening inside. But the mention of the premature death of
children, though all too frequent in times past, might suggest that Medea is now preparing to carry out her threat to kill hers. Against such
consonance of theme and dramatic expectation, the philosophic quality
of the discourse acts like counterpoint, thus heightening the suspense.

1086–1226 / 1116–1250 Sixth Episode.

1105–1201 / 1136–1230 Euripides was known for his vivid messenger speeches, conventionally used by tragedians to dramatize violent offstage action that
could not be shown in the theater to such great effect. This one is
among the best.

1113 / 1143 *princess's chambers* Wives and daughters in great houses occupied separate
quarters, where they worked and tended the younger children. Only
certain men — primarily family members — were permitted access. Others, like this messenger, were deliberately kept out.

1117 / 1147 The veil is a sign of her status as a newlywed.

1118–24 / 1149–55: It was normal for husbands to be many years older than their teenage brides. Part of a husband's duty as her new governor (*kyrios*) was to train his young bride in how to behave as the mistress of her new household.

1195–1201 / 1224–30 Another piece of proverbial wisdom from a servant; messenger speeches regularly end with them.

1199–1201 / 1228–30 A striking version of the sentiment expressed here can be found in Herodotus's tale about the reply Athenian lawgiver Solon gave to Lydian King Croesus, when he asked him whom he counted the happiest of men, thinking his own wealth and power so great that he himself would be deemed happiest. But Solon disappointed him by naming others, not nearly as rich or powerful, who had led honorable lives and then ended them in the most honorable way imaginable. According to Solon, happiness cannot be determined until a man has lived the whole of his life and cannot be equated with wealth and power. Even if a man is as rich as Croesus, he is only happy in conformity with his good luck, because at any moment his happiness can be taken away.

1227–68 / 1251–92 **Fifth Stasimon**. Throughout this ode, the agitated meter ("dochmiac") indicates an increase in the emotional intensity of the music as the play reaches its dramatic and rhetorical climax.

1227–46 / 1251–70 As witnesses to all oaths and omnipresent observers of all misdeeds, Earth and Sun are summoned to prevent an act that will activate the ineluctable Furies. In her pursuit of Jason, Medea is here depicted as one of these demonic avengers, the materialization of her own wrath which will not be appeased until she destroys his whole house, root and branch, a punishment warranted by the oath-protecting curse sworn at the time of their marriage, but one that will have grievous consequences for her, since, if she kills her children to gain the fearsome justice she seeks, she ought in turn to become the target of the new Furies awakened by the scent of her children's contaminating blood as it spreads over her hands and seeps into the ground. Indeed, among human crimes and pollutions, the shedding of kindred blood is the worst and demands compensation, no matter how long delayed, and the grace of grave purifications. Much worse than spilling an ordinary human's blood, however, is the spilling of the divinely infused blood of the gods' descendants, who have the gods themselves, not mere mortals, as their swift and sure avengers. With the words *your radiant children* (1231/1255), Euripides reminds us not only of Medea's and therefore her children's descent form Helios, but also of the fearfulness of her act and its consequences. Had Medea just avenged herself on Creon and his daughter and Jason himself, she would only have shed the foreign blood of enemies, a justifiable, though dangerous, act; but by killing her own offspring she ought to incur unspeakable cosmic retribution. Yet, in the mythical record she never does, a problem Euripides appears to dispose of at the end of the play by having Medea declare her intention of establishing a festival and expiatory rites in Corinth for her children's murder (lines 1356–1357/1381–83).

1240 / 1263 *Clashing Rocks* The Symplegades (see line 2/2).

1247–68 / 1270a–92 An offstage scream inaugurates the second system (second strophe and antistrophe) of this last choral ode, unique in that the cries of the children issuing from behind the scene building in spoken iambic verses are mixed with the singing voices of the Chorus in the orchestra. This contrast between singing and terrified shouting further heightens the agitation of the musical lines. The alternation is continued in the antistrophe, but this time the Chorus utters the unusual spoken iambic lines, which, though not screams, are nevertheless rhetorically intense.

1247 / 1273, 1252 / 1275 No matter how absurd we may find a do-nothing Chorus reacting ineffectually in song to murder and mayhem within, we must remember that this is a script for a musical and that song and dance numbers, even in our own theaters, tend to override absurdities in the action (or inaction). It is also possible that the choral dancers rendered the action more plausible through mime, for instance, by trying in vain to open the barred palace doors. Regardless of the original staging, however, standards of realism are relative, and ancient audiences who accepted rigid conventions of masks, three actors, and formal speeches in verse would not have been discomposed by passive choruses.

1259–65 / 1282–89 Ino's story is bound up in Medea's in two ways: She was the stepmother who, by persuading her husband Athamas (Jason's great uncle) to sacrifice his two children by his first wife, was the instigator of the whole saga of the Golden Fleece and its return to Greece (see Introduction, "Legendary background"). More important, her murdered son Melicertes (Palaemon), like Medea's sons at the end of the play (lines 1353–57/1378–83), became the center of a Corinthian cult. This famous "boy on a dolphin" was venerated just outside Corinth, on the shore of the isthmus, at a tomb-temple that stood within the sanctuary of Poseidon, near the race track where every fourth year the Isthmian Games were held in his honor.

After Ino's sister Semele was killed by Zeus's thunderbolt while giving birth to his son Dionysus, Ino became the infant Dionysus's wetnurse, raising him alongside her two sons by Athamas. In so doing, she incurred the anger of Hera, who drove her mad and caused her to murder her sons. After her leap into the sea, not only was Melicertes's body rescued by Poseidon's dolphin, but Ino herself was transformed into the sea nymph Leucothea, the white goddess, worshipped all over the Mediterranean basin.

Euripides wrote a tragedy called *Ino*, which recounted her persecution and transformation and was performed prior to 425 BC (cf. Aristophanes, *Acharnians* 434).

1267–68 / 1290–92, *a woman's marriage bed* The image is ambiguous in that it refers both to a woman's cravings and need for a man and a man's cravings and need for a woman. Either way, it is a fitting image to introduce Jason, who has won evils because he used the bed and a woman's lust for his own ends.

1269–end / 1293–end **Seventh Episode.**

1272 / 1297–98 *or fly on wings to heaven* Foreshadows Medea's final appearance.

1292 / 1317 To the surprise of the audience, who were probably expecting Medea and the children to be rolled out of the center door on the *eccyclema*, a platform on wheels regularly used in tragedies to display interior carnage, Medea appears above the roof of the scene building riding aloft on (or suspended from) the crane in a chariot drawn, as ancient comment and a number of vase paintings attest, by a pair of winged dragons (her own sorcerer's steeds), instead of the traditional horses of the Sun. The children's corpses must have been visibly draped on the chariot rail. The crane was a standard piece of stage equipment, the *machina* of *deus ex machina* fame from which high-flying gods often appeared abruptly at the end of Euripides' plays.

Medea's flight to Athens was enduringly etched on the ancient imagination. Eight centuries later, St. Augustine confesses (*Confessions*, 3.6) that in his pagan youth he used to sing a popular song called *Flying Medea*. (See Edith Hall, "The Singing Actors of Antiquity," in *Greek and Roman Actors*, ed. Easterling and Hall.)

1296 / 1321–22 *Helios has sent his chariot* A reminder of how well this rescue comports with Medea's dark nature as mistress of Underworld magic. After setting, the Day Star is borne on the streams of Ocean in a golden cup from west to east, where he dwells in the domain of Night with his family (Stesichorus, fr. S17=185 PMG [*ap.* Ath. 469e-f]; Parmenides DK1.9) and keeps his winged car (Mimnermus, fr. 12W [*ap.* Ath. 469f–470b]) ready to carry him aloft again at dawn through the gates of the Underworld (cf., e.g., Athenaeus, *Deipnosophistae* 469c–470d on the "cup of Heracles"). How, after a day's drive, his chariot and its steeds (whether they be horses or dragons) get back to their stalls and garage must have bothered the Greeks as well as us, for in addition to quoting earlier poets, Athenaeus cites the fifth-century Pherecydes (see note, lines 160–62/166–67) as saying that the cup carried the god *with his horses* (*ap.* Ath. 469c-d). Be that as it may, the notion of the subterranean Sun as an occult power, known to us from post-Classical Greek sources, appears to have had a firm place in fifth-century Greek thought (e.g., Peter Kingsley, *Ancient Philosophy, Mystery, and Magic*, Oxford, 1995 pp. 49 ff.). See the Introduction, "Medea's character," and notes, line 415/395–97.

1307 / 1333 *Fury* Jason says that the gods have let Medea's *alastôr* (literally, the unforgetter) fall on him by association only, thereby indicating that his children's death is really the handiwork of a demonic pursuer wreaking vengeance on Medea for her murder of her brother Apsyrtus. His own punishment, being purely accidental, is thus undeserved.

1307–9 / 1334–35 The Greek says that she killed her baby brother at her father's hearth before boarding the Argo, a version of the myth, attributed to the *Colchians*, a lost play of Sophocles. It should not be confused with the more gruesomely picturesque one attributed to Pherecydes (see note, lines 160–62/166–67). Modern readers must remind themselves of the fluidity of ancient myths, which were constantly being altered to meet the varying demands of the uses to which they were put. From her father's point of view—and from the point of view of Athenian law—this is the worst charge against Medea, that she killed her baby brother, her father's seed and heir.

1330 / 1355 *mocking me* Cf. the passages listed in the note on 401–2/383.

1350 / 1375 In the Greek, which literally says, "The terms of divorce (*apallagai*, cf. line 250/236) are easy," Jason ends more than his and Medea's shouting match.

1353–57 / 1378–83 Much like gods at the ends of other Euripidean tragedies, semi-divine Medea now sets up a causal connection between the action of the play and a real cult, in this case one established at Corinth, as expiation for her children's murder (see notes, lines 9–10/10, 1227–46/1251–70, and 1259–65/1282–89). Inasmuch as Hera was the guiding goddess of the Argo adventure, it is fitting that in death Jason's children find sanctuary in her precinct, whose location "on the heights" is perhaps to be linked to Ino's mad plunge into the sea (lines 1259–65/1282–89). Upon what heights the historical temple was founded, however, is disputed. Earlier scholars assumed it was upon Acrocorinth, the mountain above the city: archaeologists now prefer the bluffs at Perachora overlooking the Corinthian gulf. Unfortunately Pausanias, the intrepid cataloguer of the monuments of Roman Greece, saw the sacred tomb of Medea's children not in the sanctuary of Hera Akraia but near the local Music Hall, where he tells us annual rites of mourning were observed until Corinth was laid waste by the Romans (2.3.6–7).

1359–62 / 1386–88 In addition to making Jason's humiliation complete, Medea's prophecy of his death ensures that he will never beget other sons to replace the ones he has lost. In case they had forgotten, the spectators are reminded that Jason's saga ends here.

1363–end / 1389–end The Greek meter switches from spoken iambic trimeters to declaimed (i.e., Attic) anapests, a fact reflected in this translation by shorter lines. See notes, lines 86–221/96–212, 127–221/131–212.

1366 / 1392 *those who deceive their guests* Does this refer to Jason's treatment of Medea, who is a stranger and therefore a guest-friend to his house and to Greece, or to his abortive guest-friendship with Creon, or to his stealing of Aeëtes's fleece? Since Medea has just mentioned the Argo, she and the audience likely assume the last.

1370 / 1396 In Greek Medea says "Wait for old age," a statement that is not sentimental but practical. In a world without old-age pensions, children were the only means of obtaining a respectable retirement and were therefore required by Athenian law to care for their aged parents.

1392–end / 1415–end This is a stock choral tag found with slight variation at the end of four other Euripidean plays. It served to close the action but had little or no bearing on the particular play. Editors often feel compelled to bracket it to show that it is a later addition.

GLOSSARY

AEGEUS: An ancient king of Athens, primarily known as the father of Athens' founding hero, Theseus, whom, unbeknownst to him, he will soon beget in Troezen upon Pittheus's daughter Aethra. After her escape from Corinth, Medea does indeed become Aegeus's concubine and, according to one fifth-century version of her life, the mother of another son by him, Medus. When Aegeus's first son Theseus arrives in Athens to claim his birthright, she tries to do him in; but just as he is about to drink the poisoned cup, he is recognized by his father, and Medea and her son are forced to flee Athens and Greece for good.

APHRODITE: Goddess of sexual concourse, fertility, and all unions among living creatures, she was invoked primarily by brides, married women, and prostitutes, who sought from her the power to seduce men. Her literary persona, embodying beauty and feminine wiles, reflects this fact.

APOLLO: Son of Zeus and Leto, Artemis's twin brother, the multifaceted god of prophecy, music (poetry), healing, purifications, and of warrior and philosophic virtue. He is regularly depicted as a beardless youth armed with bow and arrows, the ideal of youthful male beauty. From his temple at Delphi his prophetess, the Pythia, disseminated his oracles to the Greek-speaking world.

ARGO: Jason's marvel of a ship, the world's first. Built with the goddess Athena's help and manned by intrepid pre–Trojan War heroes, it went where no Greek had gone before, from Thessaly to Colchis and home again on the quest for the Golden Fleece.

ARGONAUTS: The crew of the Argo.

ARTEMIS: A virgin huntress and mistress of wild creatures, this mighty goddess, daughter of Zeus and Leto and twin sister of Apollo, honored virginity above all other virtues and throughout Greece oversaw numerous rites of passage (sometimes bloody and cruel) from childhood to adulthood of both maidens and teenage boys. In this capacity her duties extended to aiding brides the first time they gave birth. See Hecate.

BLACK SEA (or Pontus):   Lying beyond the straits that pierce the northeast corner of the Aegean Sea, that "most wondrous of all seas" (Herodotus 4.85) was of great strategic and commercial importance for Athens, which derived a portion of its vital grain supply from its fertile hinterlands.

CEPHISUS: One of two rivers that flow around Athens, the other being the less copious Illissus.

CLASHING ROCKS: "Symplegades" in Greek, first used in this play as a name for the Cyanaean ("Blue-black") Islands at the east end of the Bosporus, which like boundary stones marked not only the entrance to the Black Sea and the western limit of contemporary Persian naval power but also, on either side of the strait, the very ends of Europe and Asia. Thus, north-south and east-west they stood between barbarians (non-Greek speakers) and Hellenes. In legend they moved together (hence "clashing"), a threat to passing ships, but became fixed after the Argo successfully sailed between them on her maiden voyage.

COLCHIS: The well-watered plain lying beneath the Caucasus Mountains at the eastern end of the Black Sea. Though Greek traders lived there in the late fifth century BC, it had a largely non-Greek population and paid tribute to the Persians. For the Greeks of that time, it still represented an eastern limit of the traveled world. Medea is referred to as "the Colchian."

CORINTH: A prosperous Greek trading city and maritime power situated on the narrow isthmus that joins the Peloponnesus to mainland Greece. Rivalry between Corinth, a Spartan ally, and Athens had often in the past led to open hostilities, which, recently reignited, had finally led to the coming war with Sparta.

CUPID: A popular Latin rendering of the Greek god Eros, a winged prepubescent boy who personified sexual desire (or *erôs*) and regularly accompanied Aphrodite. With his cruel arrows, he would strike unsuspecting victims. (See also Loves, below.)

DELPHI: Seat of Apollo's oracle on the slopes of Mount Parnassus.

EARTH: A primeval deity (Greek *Gê, Gâ, Gaia*), ancestral mother of the races of gods and men and of all living things, the firm foundation of the universe.

FURY (*erinys*: **1234**/1260 and **1363**/1389; *alastor*: **1307**/1333)/ FURIES (*miastores*: **1346**/1371): Tireless demonic avengers, embodiments of the bloody curses and unappeasable wrath of the grievously wronged, who, engorged upon the enabling, polluting blood of victims, issue from the Underworld to torture transgressors, their families, and even their cities with terrible house-destroying afflictions—disease, madness, barrenness, crop failure, and so on. Highest on their list of deserving offenders are perjurers and the slayers of kin.

GAIA: See Earth.

GOLDEN FLEECE: The fleece of a magical golden ram on whose back Phrixus escaped from death at the hands of his wicked stepmother and was carried to safety in Colchis. In gratitude to the gods, Phrixus sacrificed the ram and gave its fleece to Aeëtes, king of Aia and Medea's father. It was the mission of Jason and the Argonausts to bring the Golden Fleece back to Greece.

HARMONY: Harmonia ("fitting together") was the daughter of Aphrodite (Love) and Ares (War). As the wife of Cadmus, the mortal founder of Thebes, she became the mother of Ino (see below) and the grandmother of the wine god Dionysus.

HECATE: The menacing, nocturnal goddess associated with Artemis, Persephone, and the Moon. Accompanied by ghosts and hell-hounds and holding torches aloft, Hecate guarded the sacred entrances to the Underworld, especially at crossroads (the three ways). Through her, witches and sorcerers gained possession of their infernal, arcane knowledge.

HELIOS: The Greek word for sun, but also personified as the most powerful of the planetary deities, who daily drives his chariot westward across the sky, and during the night travels back through the Underworld to the place of his rising. When he travels the sky, he becomes the all-seeing eye of Zeus; but as a nocturnal sojourner, he is associated with the occult, and it is this dimension of his divine personality that makes him the father of Circe and Aeêtes and grandfather of Medea.

HERA: As daughter of Cronus and wife of Zeus, she was queen of the gods and goddess of marriage. Hera Akraia was the Hera who dwelled (has a cult statue) in a temple "on the heights" (*akraia*), either on Acrocorinth, the mountain above the city, or (as most archaeologists now believe) a short distance down the coast at Perachora (ancient Peraion) on bluffs overlooking the Corinthian Gulf.

HERMES: Zeus's herald, characteristically seen with a snake-wound staff (the caduceus), cap, and winged sandals. He protected travelers and children, and also guided the souls of the dead to Hades. An ingenious inventor and trickster, he made business enterprises prosper and livestock fertile. His image in the form of a talisman pillar with a head and an erect penis stood at doors throughout Athens.

INO: Daughter of Cadmus and Harmony, stepmother of Phrixus, aunt and nurse of the wine god Dionysus, she, finally, becomes the sea nymph Leukothea, who in Homer's *Odyssey* rescues raft-wrecked Odysseus off the shores of Phaeacia.

IOLCUS: A Thessalian port on the Bay of Volos at the foot of Mount Pelion, from which the legendary Argo set sail. It is Jason's hometown, ruled by his Uncle Pelias at the time of the Argo's voyage but in the action of the *Medea*, by Pelias's son Acastus.

LOVES: English for *erôtes*, the plural of Eros. Often the ardor that attends sex (*Aphrodite*) is conceptualized as a plurality.

MOUNT PELION: A mountain on the northeast border of Thessaly, at the foot of whose southwest slope lies the harbor town of Iolcus. In a cave near the mountain's peak, the mythical Centaur Chiron, tutor of heroes (including Jason), lived and taught. From its slopes the timbers of the Argo were cut.

MUSES: The daughters of Zeus and Memory who were the divine patronesses of poetry and music, learning, and the transmission of wisdom from one generation to the next.

ORPHEUS: The heroic bard was a member of Jason's crew and, according to Apollonius of Rhodes, sang at Jason's and Medea's wedding.

PAN: A wild, ithyphallic, Arcadian shepherd god, half-goat, half-manshaped, who played the syrinx (panpipes), presided over flocks and the hunting of small game, and was also credited with striking animals and men—herds, armies, and individuals—with PANics, sudden, inexplicable fears that propelled them into flight or other uncontrollable movement.

PEIRENE: A copious spring whose waters flowed into an open well in the center of Corinth, from which citizens drew their water.

PELIAS: Jason's devious uncle, ruler of Iolcus, who had sent Jason on his mission to retrieve the Golden Fleece. After the Argonauts' return, he was murdered by his daughters, who had been tricked by Medea into thinking they could rejuvenate him by adding his butchered limbs to a magical stew.

PELOPS: Eponymous hero of the Peloponnese, buried and worshipped at Olympia, he was the father of six sons, including Atreus, father of Agamemnon and Menelaus, the men who led the Greeks to Troy.

PITTHEUS: The clever ancient king of Troezen and Theseus's maternal grandfather.

SCYLLA: A terrifying, sea-dwelling she-monster first described in Homer's *Odyssey*. As Odysseus's ship passed by, each of her six doglike heads snatched one of his crew. In some later accounts she is the daughter of Hecate. By Classical times her watery lair was located in the Straits of Messina at the entrance to the Tyrrhenian (Etruscan) sea.

THEMIS: Closely associated in myth with Zeus, Themis is the divine personification of what is laid down as naturally right and holy to do, hence good order.

TROEZEN: A city in the northeast corner of the Peloponnese, overlooking the Saronic Gulf toward Athens. The two cities shared ancient ties of kinship and friendship, and it was to this place that fifty years before the *Medea* was produced the Athenians sent their wives and children when they abandoned their city to the Persians.

ZEUS: Most powerful of all the gods in the Greek pantheon, Zeus was the wise and stern king and father of the Olympian gods, ruler of the universe, and dispenser of justice. It is in his capacity as the god of justice that he is particularly invoked in this play—as the protector of suppliants and strangers, the arbiter of oaths, and the terror of wrongdoers. His thunderbolts are the invincible weapons he deploys against mortals and immortals alike who defy his will or violate divine law.

FURTHER READING

Belfiore, Elizabeth. *Murder Among Friends: Violation of* Philia *in Greek Tragedy*. Oxford, 2000; especially ch. 1, pp. 1–20.

Burnett, Anne Pippin. *Revenge in Attic and Later Tragedy*. Berkeley, CA, 1998. On *Medea*, see pp. 177–224.

Clauss, James J., and Sarah Iles Johnston, eds. *Medea: Essays on Medea in Myth, Literature, Philosophy, and Art*. Princeton, 1997.

Easterling, P. E., ed. *The Cambridge Companion to Greek Tragedy*. Cambridge, 1997.

Easterling, P. E., and Edith Hall. *Greek and Roman Actors: Aspects of an Ancient Profession*. Cambridge, 2002.

Faraone, Christopher A. "Curses and Social Control in the Law Courts of Classical Athens." *Dike* 2 (1999): 99–121.

Foley, Helene P. *Female Acts in Greek Tragedy*. Princeton, 2001; ch. III.5 "Medea's Divided Self," pp. 243–71.

Friedrich, Rainer. "Medea apolis: on Euripides' Dramatization of the Crisis of the Polis." *Tragedy, Comedy and Polis: Papers from the Greek Drama Conference, Nottingham, 18–20 July 1990*, ed. Alan H. Sommerstein et al. Bari, Italy, 1993.

Gagarin, Michael. "Women in Athenian Courts," *Dike* 1 (1998): 39–51.

Gantz, Timothy. *Early Greek Myth*. Baltimore, 1993.

Goldhill, Simon. *Reading Greek Tragedy*. Cambridge, 1986. Especially chapter on "Sexuality and Difference," 107–37.

———— "Representing Democracy: Women's Voices in Greek Literature and Society." In *Ritual, Finance, Politics*, ed. R. Osborne and S. Hornblower, festschrift for D. M. Lewis (Oxford, 1994), 347–69.

Knox, Bernard M. W. "The *Medea* of Euripides." *Yale Classical Studies* XXV: 193–225. Rpt. in Bernard M. W. Knox, *Word and Action: Essays on the Ancient Theater* (Baltimore, 1979) and in *Greek Tragedy*, ed. Erich Segal (New York, 1983).

MacDowell, Douglas M. *The Law in Classical Athens*. Ithaca, NY, 1978.

Mossman, Judith, ed. *Euripides. Oxford Readings in Classical Studies*. Oxford, 2003.

Oakley, John H., and Rebecca H. Sinos. *The Wedding in Ancient Athens*. Madison, WI, 1993.

Patterson, Cynthia. *The Family in Greek History*. Cambridge, MA, 1998.

Schaps, David M. "What Was Free about a Free Athenian Woman?" *Transactions of the American Philological Society* 128 (1998): 161–88.

Sealey, Raphael. *Women and Law in Classical Athens*. Chapel Hill, NC, 1990.

Segal, Charles. "Euripides' *Medea*: Vengeance, Reversal and Closure," *Pallas* 45 (1996): 15–44.

Wiles, David. *Tragedy in Athens: Performance Space and Theatrical Meaning*. Cambridge, 1997.